AF378697

Salvation FROM THE LAKE OF FIRE

The Beauty of John 3:16

A Layperson's Theological Perspective

Join Elisabeth in a unique, systematic journey of
defending the faith through scripture.

Discussions on:
The Three Main Views of Hell,
The Theology of a Balanced God,
Jesus' Descent to Hades,
and Is there a Postmortem Opportunity for Salvation?

ELISABETH CHRISTINE NELSON

WESTBOW
PRESS®
A DIVISION OF THOMAS NELSON
& ZONDERVAN

This book is a work of non-fiction. Unless otherwise noted, the author and the publisher make no explicit guarantees as to the accuracy of the information contained in this book and in some cases, names of people and places have been altered to protect their privacy.

WestBow Press books may be ordered through booksellers or by contacting:

WestBow Press
A Division of Thomas Nelson & Zondervan
1663 Liberty Drive
Bloomington, IN 47403
www.westbowpress.com
844-714-3454

Because of the dynamic nature of the Internet, any web addresses or links contained in this book may have changed since publication and may no longer be valid. The views expressed in this work are solely those of the author and do not necessarily reflect the views of the publisher, and the publisher hereby disclaims any responsibility for them.

Any people depicted in stock imagery provided by Getty Images are models, and such images are being used for illustrative purposes only. Certain stock imagery © Getty Images.

Interior Images, excluding Chapter 5, are by
Complete Arch Studios – Alex Gilson

ISBN: 978-1-6642-2998-3 (sc)
ISBN: 978-1-6642-2997-6 (hc)
ISBN: 978-1-6642-2999-0 (e)

Library of Congress Control Number: 2021906725

Print information available on the last page.

WestBow Press rev. date: 08/19/2021

CONTENTS

PART 3: A Biblical Overview of Eternity—With or Without God

DEDICATION

To My God

I dedicate this book to the Triune God, who led me through a spiritual journey of truth. I give Him all the glory for His divine inspiration.

To My Daughter

I dedicate this book also to my wonderful daughter, Rachel Lynn Nelson, whom I love very dearly. God truly blessed me with her.

To the Reader

As we journey together through the scriptures, I pray the blessings of the Lord be upon you, and you come to know that Jesus' sacrifice on the cross was because of His immense love for you.

ACKNOWLEDGMENTS

To Honor Those Who Assisted

I give special thanks to several persons who helped me in countless ways, especially for all their encouraging words. I appreciate everyone's contributions.

Family First

Marvin and Danalee Leadham. Both patiently listened to my early readings, ongoing updates and shared their biblical insights with me. Danalee is my mother, and Marv is her husband; my father passed away in December 2004.

Herbert and Christiana Heppner, my sister and her husband. They patiently answered my questions, shared their scriptural interpretations with me, and directed me to numerous Biblical passages.

Peter and Sharon Nelson, my brother and his wife, listened intently. My brother also pointed me to various passages, answered my endless questions, and shared his theological views.

I want to extend an additional thank you to other family members and friends. I asked them to help me select a cover image, and I had them vote on it. A majority vote went to "hands with a cross." I added the crown of thorns to remind us all that God's mercy came with a price. The helpers were: The family members above and Rachel Nelson, Andrew and Julie Nelson, Jared and Bethany Conrad, Joshua and Amanda Nelson, Danee Goodrich, and Stephen Raines.

Friends in Christ

Uche Anizor, Ph.D., Associate Professor of Theology, Talbot Theological Seminary at Biola University (La Mirada, California), and author of numerous books and articles. Anizor evaluated part of my manuscript and offered valuable critiques.

Kenneth Berding, whom I first met at church. He was teaching a Sunday School class on the *Gifts of the Spirit.* Berding encouraged me from the very beginning and kept me on target. Berding reviewed part of my manuscript and shared his constructive theological comments.

Robert Bishop, Lead Pastor, Redemption Hill Church (Whittier, California). In the beginning, Pastor Bishop encouraged me with my journey, which inspired the theme for my book.

Stephen G. Raines, D.Min., Pastor, Lakeview Missionary Baptist Church in Mena, Arkansas. Raines retired in July 2020 after sixteen years of teaching as an Assistant Professor (Social Studies Department), Central Baptist College, Arkansas. Raines is a former high school classmate from American Heritage Christian Schools (Hayward, California). He encouraged me along the way, recommended scriptural references, reviewed part of my manuscript, and offered his words of wisdom.

I want to extend an extra thank you to the young woman at work who openly shared her strong faith in Jesus Christ. She permitted me to share our conversations within the book if it would help others. Even though we disagree on certain biblical subjects, we respect each other's thoughts and appreciate our engaging discussions to this very day.

I express my gratitude and appreciation for whom I had conversations with, whether at church, work, online, or family gatherings, regarding my book's research questions.

Thanks to you all! I could not have done it without you—it took a village!

A Tribute to American Heritage Christian Schools

I would like to honor American Heritage Christian Schools, Hayward, California. The school opened its doors in the Fall of 1968 and closed its doors in May 2005. Initially, the school campus was at Fairway Park Baptist Church, and the school's superintendent was the pastor of the church, Rev. Elliott T. Paulsen. Rev. Paulsen was a dedicated minister and a strong advocate for the school. I am not sure of the year, but I learned that Rev. Paulsen is with the Lord. Through Internet research, it appeared the school moved (not certain of the exact year) to a different location before closing its doors.

We had a football team and a cheerleading squad, which I was on. I was also Vice President of the student council during the time I attended (1968–1970). My father was in between pastoral church assignments, so he joined the faculty at American Heritage. I had my father as a geometry and English teacher. And, no, he did not show favoritism. Two of my siblings also attended this school. My mother painted the school signage, including drawing and painting the school mascot, the Bald Eagle. My father accepted a new church assignment in Citrus Heights (near Sacramento), California, so our family moved in the Spring of 1970.

I usually did not care for history classes; however, I did like the class, Rudiments of our American Government. This class taught the real history of our country. The following definitions are from the 1969 and 1970 yearbooks. First, rudiments taught us "perceiving the history of Christianity and America as inseparable and requisite to understanding the relation of individual character to a nation's government."[1] Second, the government class was a "study of the American Christian constitutional form of government and the idea of liberty with law."[2] Further, the History class was "a study of Christ: His story, the westward movement of Christianity, Christian liberty, government, and individual character as contrasted with the pagan and socialistic story."[3]

Additionally, these three main principles were taught:

- God's Principle of Individuality
- For every ounce of freedom, there is an ounce of responsibility
- One person's rights end when another's begin

I highly doubt our American public-school system teaches those philosophies, including the three principles. For most of my school life, I attended public schools, which were excellent [at that time], but they did not teach those values listed above.

---

[1] Rudiments, definition taken from American Heritage Christian Schools yearbook, 1969.

[2] Government, Ibid.

[3] History, definition taken from American Heritage Christian Schools yearbook, 1970.

For example, God and prayer used to be in our public schools. When I was in kindergarten, we prayed before our milk and graham crackers and then took our naps. Also, I remember when I graduated from eighth grade, the public school, Porter Elementary (Alameda, California), asked my father to pray before our graduation picnic party. Imagine that!

To all the past students and faculty of American Heritage Christian Schools—Go Team Go! I miss you all.

An Invitation to a Journey

I, Elisabeth C. Nelson,

personally invite you

to take a journey through

scripture with me.

As we progress through

the pages of His Word,

we will learn together

the truth of God's message

to every person.

PART ONE

A Biblical Overview for Spiritual Growth

A STATEMENT OF BIBLICAL THEOLOGY

I cannot express enough the extreme importance of God's message to all humanity. The heart of the message of God's holy Word is this.

- God wants a personal and spiritually intimate relationship with each of us because He loves us "very dearly" (John 16, John 16:27 NLT).
- God proved that love by sending His only begotten Son, Jesus Christ, to earth to take the sins of the world upon Himself and die on the cross, Calvary's tree, and shed His precious blood to offer all humanity the gift of salvation (John 3:16; 1 Peter 1:18–21).
- This sacrificial act of love was completed ("It is finished," John 19:30) because humanity has been in a state of condemnation since Adam and Eve fell into sin in the Garden of Eden (Genesis 3:17–19, Romans 5:12). Thus, humanity needs redemption. Furthermore, the initial sin of disobedience broke the relationship between God and humanity. Therefore, no one can come before God the Father except through Jesus Christ (John 14:6; Revelation 21:27).

- Jesus' sacrificial act of love bridges the gap of the broken relationship.
- Humankind has been denying and rejecting God and has unbelief in Him, the theology of condemnation, and the refusal of redemption.
- Humankind has also refused to believe in [the existence of] the spiritual warfare between good and evil—God and Satan (Ephesians 6).

- Without redemption, each person's soul's eternal destination will be in the lake of fire (Daniel 12:2, Matthew 25:46; John 5:29; 2 Thessalonians 1:8–9; Revelation 20:14–15). If the lake of fire were complete annihilation or temporary punishment, there would be no need for God's sacrificial love for humanity.
- Jesus died on the cross because there is a lake of fire with an eternal judgment that He wanted to save us from because He loves us. If there were no eternal lake of fire to save us from, Jesus would have died in vain.
- We need to understand the following concepts.
  - In a lost and broken world, all individuals need salvation.
  - A soul's eternal destination is either heaven or hell.
  - Only through Jesus Christ can we receive salvation as a free-will choice.

We have an enemy who wants us to think that our physical death is the end of our life; however, scriptures tell us the opposite. The Christian faith is set apart and above all others due to the biblical facts that Jesus was born of a virgin (Matthew 1:23, 25; Luke 1:27, 34), died (John 19:30), was raised from the dead (Romans 10:9, Acts 4:10), and sits at the right hand of God (Mark 16:19, Romans 8:34). Jesus is the Son of God and the son of man, and He is the "Incarnate Word" (1 John 1:1–3 NASB).

The biblical fact of eternal punishment in the lake of fire (Daniel 12:2; Matthew 13:41–42; 25:41, 46; John 5:29; Revelation 12:10, 20:15) is set apart and above all others due to the deep-rooted spiritual fact of what Jesus did on the cross; "My grace is sufficient for you" (2 Corinthians 12:9 NASB). The philosophies of complete annihilation, temporary punishment, or other non-biblical views devalue and diminish what Jesus did on the cross and diminishes the magnitude of sin.

Let's start our journey together.

SPIRITUAL EDIFICATION—A FIRM FOUNDATION

An Overview

I feel this world is spiritually lost and blind to the truth of God's Word. In Matthew 9:36–38 (NASB), we read how Jesus "felt compassion for the people." In Matthew 9:37 (NASB), Jesus told His disciples, "The harvest is plentiful, but the workers are few." Through this book, I pray that I am "one of those few workers" by sharing what I have learned.

My intentions are not to offend anyone. I am not being critical or judging anyone's beliefs. Instead, I want to share what I have learned so that we can learn together the truth of God's Word.

Throughout this book, I made great efforts to scripturally document and support the theology I have presented. I diligently gave credit where credit was due. The opposing opinions and views of those I quoted, I respected and accepted their words as an education.

Some subjects I will be addressing are complicated and sensitive and may appear to be harsh and critical, but my goal is to help others understand the truth of God's Word, which is not always easy. Therefore, I have compassionately presented the material in a straightforward and matter-of-fact methodology to offer easy-to-comprehend Biblical theology without mincing God's word.

I pray I can use my gift of simplification of a challenging subject with respect and reverence. Stephen Raines, a former classmate from American Heritage Christian Schools, reminded me of the following passage.

> But in your hearts honor Christ the Lord as holy, always being prepared to make a defense to anyone who asks you for a reason for the hope that is in you; yet do it with gentleness and respect. (1 Peter 3:15 ESV)

I conducted training meetings for two of the companies that I worked for in the past. I was able to break down complicated subjects so all could understand them. I heard comments such as, "Before the training, my stress level was sky high." After the training, I heard, "Elisabeth, you made everything seem so easy, and my stress level dropped, and I could breathe." So, while I was deciding to write this book, I thought, *Why not use my gift for the Lord?*

The Word of God

> All Scripture is inspired by God and beneficial for teaching, for rebuke, for correction, for training in righteousness; so that the man *or woman* of God may be fully capable, equipped for every good work. (2 Timothy 3:16–17 NASB)

For the word of God is living and active and sharper than any two-edged sword, even penetrating as far as the division of soul and spirit, of both joints and marrow, and able to judge the thoughts and intentions of the heart. (Hebrews 4:12 NASB)

One primary purpose of this book is to reach out to people with the truth of God's Word. Yes, indeed, the Word of God cuts to the core of our very being. The scripture itself sometimes appears to be harsh and lacks sensitivity; however, we must understand that God's Word speaks only the truth and that there are times when the truth hurts and may be difficult to understand.

God's Word cuts to our very being, but it also expresses quite extensively His love for us, which is especially spelled out in the book of John. Chapter 16 tells us that the Father loves us dearly (NLT), and in Chapter 15, Jesus said that He is the vine, and we are the branches. And of course, in John 3 is the favorite verse of all—John 3:16. This verse tells us that God does indeed love us because He sent His Son, Jesus, to die for our sins and save us.

✓ Key verses: John 3:16, 15:5, 16:27

In Today's Uncertain Turbulent Times

I want to take a moment to address our current troubled culture worldwide because of the Covid-19 Pandemic. Who knew we would be wearing face masks during our lifetime? We might wonder *where God is during this time.* Additionally, we may question why we did not get the job we wanted, why didn't the house deal go through, or why did someone break off a relationship after many years? We may never know those answers, or perhaps, we may find out later in life, as I have discovered. For example, I went to a job interview several years ago and thought I was a "shoe-in;" however, I was not offered the position. About five years later, I learned the company went out of business five months after my interview. I learned through that circumstance that God was watching out for me.

The current pandemic is far worse than other situations we may have experienced or will encounter. I learned the following in my studies, not sure where, so I do not take credit for this: We also need to realize that God allows events to take place to deal with humanity's sinful nature. The Bible covers this quite well, as you will note throughout this book. God sees things quite differently than we do, and He deals with them quite differently than we think He should. God does answer prayer in His time, not our time. He sees in the future and answers our prayers for our best and to glorify Him. The ultimate result God desires is "not willing for any to perish, but for all to come to repentance" (2 Peter 3:8–9 NASB).

In the book *30 Life Principles*, Charles Stanley addresses this relevant issue.

> Life Principle 9 teaches: *Trusting God means looking beyond what we can see to what God sees.* The circumstances and obstacles that you observe today may be truly overwhelming, but God's resources are even greater and more

powerful than you can imagine. God knows what is ahead and He is ready to deal with it. Therefore, put your faith in Him and obey whatever He says.[4]

Stanley hit the spiritual nail on the head regarding this subject. In his book, Stanley used scripture from 2 Kings 6:8–23 regarding enemies surrounding Elisha, and his servant, being afraid, could not see that God was protecting them.

> And Elisha prayed, "Open his eyes, Lord, so that he may see." Then the Lord opened the servant's eyes, and he looked and saw the hills full of horses and chariots of fire all around Elisha. (2 Kings 6:17 NIV)

I understand that it may be challenging to comprehend why God has allowed the pandemic to overwhelm our lives, and in some cases, has taken many lives. However, we all need to recognize the important things: God is in control, and He loves us. God's Word assures us:

> The LORD is close to the brokenhearted; he rescues those whose spirits are crushed. (Psalms 34:18 NLT)

---

[4] Charles F. Stanley, *30 Life Principles* (Nashville: Thomas Nelson, 2008), 43.

A Prayer: Lord, I pray for healing for the families that have lost someone due to Covid-19 or other medical issues. I ask in Jesus' name that you bring them peace and hope as they emotionally heal. Please assure them of your love. In Jesus' name, Amen.

Spiritual Warfare

There is spiritual warfare in this world, and it is real. Most people live day after day going places and doing things unaware of the spiritual warfare surrounding them. People get ready for work and think about what to eat, whom to marry, what car to buy, and so on, but are they concerned about what happens after death? Do they think about how to live their lives purposely? It is essential for us to set a course of purpose in our lives.

We need to stand firm in Christ and who He has made us to be. Satan is real, and he is <u>evil</u>; never forget that. You will never <u>outsmart</u> Satan. To be part of the Kingdom of God, it is inevitable that a person will experience a spiritual attack; if it has not happened to you yet, it will.[5]

---

[5] Paraphrased from Lead Pastor Robert Bishop's sermon "Standing Firm with the Armor of God," (Redemption Hill Church, September 1, 2019).

I heard the above from Pastor Robert Bishop's sermon on Sunday, September 1, 2019, "Stand Firm with the Armor of God." Bishop continued to share this.

If we keep ignoring the spiritual warfare, then we have already lost. Do not despair. There is hope. As Christians, we have the power of prayer: <u>never</u> forget that either. Do not try to solve difficulties on your own. It does not mean we cannot use our knowledge to get out of a situation; however, we need to pray first and ask the Lord to lead us in the right direction. (Paraphrased)[6]

Ephesians 6:11 (NASB) tells us, "Put on the full armor of God, so that you will be able to stand firm against the schemes of the devil."

> ✓ Key verses: Ephesians 6:13, 4:14; Romans 13:12; James 4:7; 1 Thessalonians 5:8. Main sermon passage: Ephesians 6:10–24.

Spiritual warfare surrounds us and affects our entire world. For reflection, we usually gain the most spiritual growth in our Christian walk during seasons of adversity. The outsiders do not seem to view things the way God does. Our world deals with dark issues, such as homosexuality, abortion, and socialism, just to name a few. The benefits we have as Christians are that we have the power of prayer, God's Word, and the Holy Spirit's help to guide us and protect us. Just remember these words from our Lord.

---

[6] Paraphrased from Lead Pastor Robert Bishop's sermon "Standing Firm with the Armor of God," (Redemption Hill Church, September 1, 2019).

These things I have spoken to you so that in Me you may have peace. In the world you have tribulation, but take courage; I have overcome the world. (John 16:33 NASB)

The unbelievers need our aid, and that is why we need to share the Gospel of Jesus Christ—following the Great Commission.

Standing Firm

Stand firm in your faith by stamping your foot down to sin. Strive to live your life in God's will and even under your roof with yourself and your family. That can be difficult to do [at times] because believers and unbelievers alike seem to accept some worldly feelings, beliefs, or even emotions as not sinful. Humanity takes various lifestyles as normal; however, the Bible warns us not to do detestable, evil things in the sight of the Lord (KJV: 2 Kings 17:13; Jeremiah 4:1, 18:11). Additionally, Revelation describes for us the following.

Outside are the dogs and sorcerers and the sexually immoral and murderers and idolaters, and everyone who loves and practices falsehood. (Revelation 22:15 ESV)

California's public-school system and in some other States teach first graders through college that same-sex relationships and marriages are normal. To clarify the matter, I would like to interject that what is taught is that same-sex sexual relationships are normal. Because same-gender relationships, such as platonic friendships, are perfectly fine and natural. I learned that teachers are not allowed to say anything negative about same-sex sexual relationships, not even warning about HIV or AIDS health issues related to that lifestyle. The instructors are not to discuss any biblical differences either. This teaching method makes it difficult for Christian parents to instruct their children because they are receiving conflicting information at school. To my best understanding, there is current legislation fighting this. One resource is the Pacific Justice Institute (pji. org). Christians are taking a stand against this teaching in our public schools. I feel that this is one-sided teaching, which is not fair, right, or correct. I think public schools should teach both viewpoints.

The Bible is clear regarding same-sex sexual relationships and marriages, and further, we are to teach sound doctrine. If you are curious, please check out Leviticus 18:22, 20:13, 1 Corinthians 6:9, 1 Timothy 1:9–11, 2 Timothy 4:3, and Titus 1:9 (ESV explains it best). Jesus tells us, "Make them holy by your truth; teach them your word, which is truth" (John 17:17 NLT). Yet, our teachers instruct our children's minds (via the school board's criteria) with ungodly lusts. Homosexuality is Biblically considered ungodly, lustful, and sinful. Scripture tells us, "In the last time there will be mockers, following after their own ungodly lusts. These are the ones who cause divisions, worldly-minded, devoid of the Spirit" (Jude 1:18–19 NASB).

The decision of instructing our children with only one viewpoint lends to telling our children how and what they should think. Instead, the school should offer a Biblical perspective for our children to think on their own—make their own independent decisions after hearing both sides. Wasn't there a Christian or two on the school board? I would think that the school board would want to instruct our precious young minds with information that would positively assist them throughout their lives, not fill their minds with sinful worldly concepts.

> Or do you not know that the unrighteous will not inherit the kingdom of God? Do not be deceived; neither the sexually immoral, nor idolaters, nor adulterers, nor homosexuals, nor thieves, nor *the* greedy, nor those habitually drunk, nor verbal abusers, nor swindlers, will inherit the kingdom of God. (1 Corinthians 6:9–10 NASB)

Indeed, we need to offer age-related information at every grade level. As the students learn the truth they can understand, their knowledge will increase at every grade level. I feel deeply saddened for the teachers who are Christian. They would lose their jobs if they taught our children the Biblical truth about same-sex sexual relationships. Additionally, if a law is contrary to scripture, then the ruling is wrong.

It is also challenging to stamp your foot down to sin in a divided household. There are times when an unbeliever becomes a believer. Thus, the spiritual warfare begins because an unbeliever has difficulty understanding the religious change in a family member. Such was the situation in *The Case for Christ* by Lee Strobel. Here is a summary: Strobel and his wife were both atheists until his wife became a believer. Strobel tells his story; he contemplated divorce, but he saw the light and became a believer during his journalistic investigation of trying to prove there was no God.[7]

We are not to be "unequally yoked" with nonbelievers. Paul was speaking to the Corinthians on this matter in 2 Corinthians 6:14–15. It is not just in marriages but in any relationship we have. It does not mean we are cruel to unbelievers; we are to love them, pray for them, and show them the light of Jesus through how we live. For example, in a workplace environment, we may be employed by an unbeliever. We need to show the light of Jesus through us and view the job as a missionary assignment.

Additionally, it does not mean that if we are married to unbelievers that we divorce them—certainly not. Instead, we should love them, pray for them, and live our lives in such a way that they see the light of Jesus through us—"walk as children of the light" (Ephesians 5:8 NASB). This task of love may be challenging because we are not perfect. However, the following scripture helps us understand how to stand firm.

> Whereunto he called you by our gospel, to the obtaining of the glory of our Lord Jesus Christ. Therefore, brethren, stand fast, and hold the traditions which ye have been taught, whether by word, or our epistle. Now our Lord Jesus Christ himself, and God, even our Father, which hath loved us, and hath given us everlasting consolation and good hope through grace. (2 Thessalonians 2:14–16 KJV)

---

[7] Lee Strobel, *The Case for Christ* (Grand Rapids: Zondervan, 1998, 2016).

The Bible: Our Manual for Living

It is essential to understand that the Bible is our manual for life and how to live it. The Bible also shows us how we learn about God's Blueprint for our lives and how He uses adversity to help us spiritually mature. Here are excerpts from Kenneth Berding's book *Bible Revival.* Berding wrote about two foundational beliefs about the Bible.[8]

1. All things needed for life and godliness are *here in the Bible.*
2. All things needed for life and godliness are *clear in the Bible.*

Berding further explains for us:

> I am not saying that the Bible comments on every piece of knowledge ever discovered, nor am I saying that every verse in the Bible is equally clear. But I want to shamelessly assert that all things we need for life and godliness are here in the Bible and all things we need for life and godliness are clear in the Bible.[9]

Berding shares what the scriptures say to us about God and Salvation:

> 2 Peter 1:3–4 speaks to the value of the Bible in the context of all that God has given us for

---

[8] Kenneth Berding, *Bible Revival: Recommitting Ourselves to One Book* (Bellingham, WA: Lexham Press, 2013), 32.

[9] Ibid., 32.

salvation and growth in knowing him…In short, the all-powerful God has made available to us everything we need to come to salvation and to live godly lives that please him. We live the lives he has prepared for us and grow in godliness as we come to know Jesus Christ via the incredible promises given to us in the Bible.[10]

Throughout our life, God uses struggles and trials to help us spiritually grow and become strong and knowledgeable in His Word; thus, making us more effective as Christians, which shows us that God does love us and wants the best for us. The parable of the "Little Tea Cup" will guide you through a little side trip to an antique shop, which I am sure will show you God's love for you—even despite life's adversities. I would advise you to bring a box of tissues with you. The following is the Internet link:

jennysthread.com/the-parable-of-the-little-tea-cup - Bing

Did you brew yourself a cup of tea? What are your thoughts? Have there been events in your life that you did not know why they happened? After reading the story, were you able to relate those events to God's purpose for your life? Scripture helps us to understand that God is our potter, and we are the clay.

But now, LORD, You are our Father; We are the clay, and You our potter, And all of us are the work of Your hand. (Isaiah 64:8 NASB)

---

[10] Berding, *Bible Revival, 33.*

The Bible further informs us that we are to pray without ceasing (Ephesians 6:18), and we are to anticipate Jesus' return (1 John 3:2–3). I know the above is just a brief description of biblical application. I hope this helps you in your journey in a meaningful way.

Spiritual Discernment

When we become followers of Jesus Christ, a beautiful thing occurs—the Holy Spirit moves into our lives. Jesus explained to His disciples that after He rose from the dead and ascended to heaven, He would send a helper, meaning He would not abandon them.

> But I tell you the truth, it is to your advantage that
> I am leaving; for if I do not leave, the Helper will
> not come to you; but if I go, I will send Him to you.
> (John 16:7 NASB)

The Holy Spirit is not only our helper; He is also our teacher—"For the Spirit teaches you everything you need to know" (1 John 2:27 NLT). Without writing another book or creating another chapter, the Holy Spirit does not control us because we are not puppets or robots. One of the roles of the Holy Spirit is to transform us into being more Christ-like. I cherish the knowledge the Holy Spirit brings to my mind; it is an incredible experience. Also, read John 14:16–17, 26: "The Helper is the Spirit of truth" (v 17a NASB).

As I will discuss throughout my book, God gave us all free will. God also gave the angels He created free will. Hence,

Lucifer and his band of followers (fallen angels), now known as demons, used that free will and wanted to become gods themselves, but they were cast out of heaven; consequently, the spiritual warfare began. Lucifer, now Satan, is still beautiful, and he does an excellent job of making sin look enticing. That is why we need to be grounded in the Word of God. We need to listen to our helper, the Holy Spirit. Sometimes, the Holy Spirit speaks softly, and we need to pay attention.

As we mature in our walk with the Lord, we develop spiritual discernment by praying, reading the Bible, and asking the Holy Spirit to guide us. It is amazing how scripture seems to jump up at us when we ask the Holy Spirit's help to understand what we are reading. I love that!

We need to make sure, however, that we are listening to the right spirit. We can be divinely inspired, but God will never give us new revelation. The Holy Bible, God's Word, is "the new revelation;" therefore, there is no new revelation. If we believe God has given us new insights, but it is contrary to the Holy Bible, it did not come from God—it came from Satan. God will never tell us anything opposite from His Word! Remember, Satan is a big deceiver, and he loves to mince God's words— look what happened to Eve in the Garden of Eden (Genesis 2:17; 3:4–6). We can be given enlightenment, divine inspiration, or clarification through the Holy Spirit, but it will not be a new revelation. "But if any of you lacks wisdom, let him ask of God, who gives to all generously and without reproach, and it will be given to him" (James 1:5 NASB).

Always open your Bible and look to see if what you heard matches the Word of God; this is where discernment comes in. Always check out the source!

Beloved, do not believe every spirit, but test the spirits to see whether they are from God, for many false prophets have gone out into the world. By this you know the Spirit of God: every spirit that confesses that Jesus Christ has come in the flesh is from God, and every spirit that does not confess Jesus is not from God. This is the spirit of the Antichrist, which you heard was coming and now is in the world already. (1 John 4:1–3 ESV)

But you belong to God, my dear children. You have already won a victory over those people, because the Spirit who lives in you is greater than the spirit who lives in the world. Those people belong to this world, so they speak from the world's viewpoint, and the world listens to them. (1: John 4:4–5 NLT)

Please be cautious with what are called contemplative prayer, transcendental meditation, and guided prayer. Repeating mantras is not taught in the Bible, nor are the other items I just mentioned. However, if guided prayer is done, such as saying we will pray for our president, grandma, and the like, that is okay. Yet if people are sitting in yoga or similar positions muttering mantras, we need to be careful, as we may get into Eastern religions, which Jesus did not teach. Yoga itself is a religion and is spiritual, but it is not Christian.

Let's discuss the Lord's Prayer. Jesus never meant for the Lord's Prayer to be repetitive or done in a mantra-like manner, and He considered it to be pagan to do so (Matthew 6:7–8).

Instead, Jesus wanted our prayer to be customized. Therefore, he shared the Lord's Prayer with us to outline what prayer should include. The Lord's Prayer is indeed essential, and it should never be devalued. However, here is another way to look at it: "You don't say prayers, you pray prayers."[11] This quote comes from the book *When We Say Father.* The authors spiritually break down the Lord's Prayer for us, which provides a deeper understanding of what Jesus is trying to teach us through this prayer.

I feel we do not give the Holy Spirit enough credit. He is part of the Trinity, and we should be paying attention to His spiritual nudges. Some people call the Holy Spirit their conscience. He is a lot more than just that, but that is a good start. The Holy Spirit is instrumental in assisting us with our prayers. We need to tap into the Holy Spirit's help in our prayer life, for there are times we need to pray, yet we do not know precisely how to pray. The scriptures inform us of the following.

> In the same way the Spirit also helps our weakness; for we do not know how to pray as we should, but the Spirit Himself intercedes for *us* with groanings too deep for words. (Romans 8:26 NASB)

> Praying always with all prayer and supplication in the Spirit, and watching thereunto with all perseverance and supplication for all saints. (Ephesians 6:18 KJV)

––––––––––––

[11] Stephen M. Rogers and Adrian Rogers, *When We Say Father* (Nashville: B&H Publishing Group, © 2018), 1. Reprinted and used by permission.

Remember that sin is evil, and Satan is evil, and he loves to deceive people, especially Christians. He wants to dishearten us and sway us away from God. So, Jesus warned us about Satan: "Whenever he tells a lie, he speaks from his own *nature*, because he is a liar and the father of lies" (John 8:44 NASB).

Because people continue to absorb themselves in wickedness, they start believing in false doctrines, turn a blind eye to God's truth, and refuse salvation. "For this reason God will send upon them a deluding influence so that they will believe what is false, in order that they all may be judged who did not believe the truth, but took pleasure in wickedness" (2 Thessalonians 2:11–12 NASB).

Some claim they know God but have allowed worldly corruption to flow into their minds tainting their thinking process, which translates into how they live their lives. The Book of Titus explains, "Everything is pure to those whose hearts are pure. But nothing is pure to those who are corrupt and unbelieving, because their minds and consciences are corrupted. Such people claim they know God, but they deny him by the way they live. They are detestable and disobedient, worthless for doing anything good" (Titus 1:15–16 NLT).

On a more positive note, be not dismayed; there is hope because God does indeed love us! Jesus sacrificed Himself for all of us by shedding His precious blood and dying on the cross if we will only receive Him of our own free will.

> For God so loved the world that he gave his only begotten Son, that whosoever believeth in Him should not perish but have everlasting life. (John 3:16 KJV)

Spiritual Awareness Questions

Jesus asked His disciples, "'Who do you say that I am?' Peter answered and said to Him, 'You are the Christ'" (Mark 8:29 NASB).

✓ See also Matthew 16:15; Luke 9:20

If Jesus Christ asked you that question, what would your response be?

Is your name in the Book of Life? What does your eternity look like?

The following passage is speaking of who will enter the Kingdom of God.

Nothing impure will enter it, nor will anyone who does what is shameful or deceitful, but only those whose names are written in the Lamb's Book of life. (Revelation 21:27 NIV)

If you need time to ponder, that is okay. As you journey with me, perhaps you will discover your answers along the way. I will ask the same questions later.

BACKGROUND—THE INSPIRATION

I often wonder why people write books or articles; you know—What inspired them? So, let me share with you how it all began with me.

Conversations I have had regarding faith in God led me to conduct some Internet research. One such conversation was with a young woman at work. The focus of one of our discussions was regarding the Trinity. She had disbelief in the Trinity, but she believed in God, Jesus, and the Holy Spirit but not as one at the same time.

My goal was to share articles from the Internet and passages from the Bible to prove that the Trinity was real. I typed in the word *Trinity*, and several websites popped up. As I was reviewing them, I noticed an array of scripturally sound articles on one particular website, such as the Deity of Jesus and the Trinity.

Then I saw articles on hell. As I was reading the first one, I sensed something that did not feel right. Whistles, bells, and red flags were going off in my mind, making me feel uneasy. I had the feeling that the information was perhaps not scriptural; this is where spiritual discernment through the Holy Spirit is helpful.

I stopped reading for a while and started to pray. I asked God to give me discernment as I read the balance of the article.

While I was praying, I asked God, "Have I believed wrong all my life?" I asked the question because the words I was reading were compelling, yet I was feeling uneasy. God gave me peace of mind as I finished reading.

The first article concluded that the lake of fire was not eternal punishment or judgment; it was complete annihilation.[12] The article shocked me because some of the other articles on that website were scripturally sound. Please understand me, that was not the first time I had heard of this philosophy, yet I had not heard of the term conditionalism. I know of a religion that believes that evil souls just die. Then, I decided to read some of the other articles on other sites to see their conclusions. Even though the various authors believed there was a lake of fire, from my understanding of the Bible, the conclusion of complete annihilation was not scripturally sound. With additional searching, I soon learned about Universalism, which teaches the lake of fire is a purification process to reconcile with God for those who die as unbelievers. These views will be discussed in greater depth in Chapter 1.

At that point, I first learned about conditionalism and universalism. The idea of complete annihilation or reconciling with God after death is not theologically correct—it is a man's philosophy, not God's. *So how do I prove that?* I asked myself. More precisely, *how do I prove that through scripture and in an engaging way?*

I thought about the articles for about two to three weeks and continued my research, but I focused on materials and books on hell, the lake of fire, God's attributes, and of course,

---

[12] Jeremy K. Moritz, *Hell: Eternal Torment or Complete Annihilation?* 2003. Website: Truth According to Scripture.

the Bible. I asked questions of my pastor, family members, and church friends.

To make the conclusions plausible, two things must be. Either the Bible lies or contradicts itself, and sin goes unpunished—no consequences. Additionally, Satan, demons, the Antichrist, the false prophet, those who took the mark, and those whose names are not in the Book of Life will just die, or they all go through a purification process. I do not believe the Bible teaches that Satan, etc., will be purified. In all fairness, I do not think the Universalists believe that Satan, etc., will be purified either. However, since the Bible says Satan will be thrown into the lake of fire and so will unbelievers, and if the lake of fire is a purification process, what will happen to Satan?

Grounded in the Word of God

It is essential to read the Word of God daily, as it helps us discern which doctrines are true or not true. In other words, when we read God's Word daily, it allows our minds to sift and screen other materials we read—does it match the Word of God? Please refer to 1 Timothy 4:6, "*constantly* nourished" (NASB), and Titus 1:9, "holding firmly the faithful word" (NASB).

Examine the Word of God for yourself. Our pastors and other Christian leaders are our guides through scripture and essential for our Christian growth. So, please take the following sentence with *a grain of salt* (and perhaps a *slight* sense of humor): Do not believe me, your pastor, Christian articles, or what you hear on the Christian radio stations—check things out for yourself. This principle is what Apostle Paul was trying to explain to us in the Book of Acts. Paul and Silas were traveling to Berea, "and when they arrived, they went into the Jewish synagogue. Now these Jews were more noble than those in Thessalonica, they received the word with all eagerness, examining the scriptures daily to see if these things were so" (Acts 17:10–11 ESV).

Even though I disagreed with the conclusions of the various authors of Conditionalism and Universalism, I did find their articles professionally written. Of course, people may disagree with each other; however, we should value and respect one another's opinions and thoughts.

My new quest in life was to research, document, discover the truth, and see where it led me. Let's continue our journey and find the answers together.

INTRODUCTION—THE START OF A JOURNEY

An Overview

This book is written with the faith and trust that God's Holy Word is true, does not contradict itself, is inspired by God, stands forever, and is the unchanging living Word of God (NASB: 2 Timothy 3:16–17; Isaiah 40:8; Hebrews 4:12; 13:8; John 1:1–5).

Our God is an unchanging God, and scripture assures us of this fact.

> Every good gift and every perfect gift is from above, coming down from the Father of lights, with whom there is no variation or shadow due to change. (James 1:17 ESV)

Is your name written in the Book of Life?

There is nothing more important than our salvation—Nothing! Therefore, we should be extremely careful about what we spiritually believe in because our souls' eternal destination depends on it. Whether we have a relationship with Jesus Christ or not when we take our last breath will determine our souls' eternal destination.

The above statement is essential and inclusive to spreading the Gospel of Jesus Christ to redeem the world; therefore, nothing is more important than everyone's salvation.

A Little About Myself

I wrote this book from a layperson's theological perspective, with the intent to reach out to people with God's message of love and redemption. However, I am a theologian at heart, and I want to share what I have learned in a simplified format and using well-supported biblical references.

I do not hold a degree in theology, so I had to remind myself that the first few disciples Jesus chose were ordinary fishermen. Jesus asked them to be fishers of men (Matthew 4:19; Mark 1:17). I also felt led by the Holy Spirit to share my journey to discovering the truth of God's Word with others to equip them in their mission of pursuing godly lives.

> For we are God's handiwork, created in Christ Jesus to do good works, which God prepared in advance for us to do. (Ephesians 2:10 NIV)

I was born and raised in a strict Christian Baptist home and the oldest of five children. We were all taught Christian theology from the cradle on up, even at the dinner table. There were many times the dinner table became a classroom. When we did not understand an idea, a theological subject, or how to spell a word, our father told us, "look it up." Then out would come a dictionary, an encyclopedia, or the Bible. When I was nine, I accepted the Lord as my personal Savior at a Billy Graham crusade in Fresno, California. When I was in seventh grade, my father became an ordained Baptist minister. My brothers, my sisters, and I were then PKs, preacher's kids. I attended a private Christian school, American Heritage Christian Schools, in Hayward, California, for two of my high school years.

I currently consider myself a Baptist, but I am a Christian first. The Christian faith is the true faith, not particularly a church affiliation. When I was much younger, I ventured out and explored other religions and beliefs. After examining them, I decided that I wanted to worship at a Baptist church. Please understand, there are varying beliefs among the Baptists, as with other types of churches. In other words, I would not attend just any Baptist church; I would examine their Statement of Faith. The current church I attend had a name change a few years ago, which does not reflect Baptist in its title. However, the church continues to teach the Baptist doctrines fundamentally. Therefore, ensure that whatever church you worship has a Statement of Faith in line with God's Word.

U-Turns

I humbly confess that I have not always lived my life as a Christian should; I have had a journey of my own. God has taken me through many painful learning lessons throughout my life because of some decisions and choices I made. I had slowly moved from the narrow path to the broad road of destruction (Matthew 7:13–14). It was not until later in life; I moved back to the narrow path. I am a living testimony that God does allow U-Turns in your life—just do not let them pass you up. While you are alive, you have the opportunity to jump over to the narrow path to heaven's gate. God also showed me the silver lining in those stormy clouds of adversities. Some of you may be experiencing turbulent waters, such as battling health issues or perhaps in an abusive relationship, whether personal or work-related. Just remember, nothing is too complicated for our Lord (Jeremiah 32:17).

Scripture offers us hope. Psalms 107:27–29 talks about a storm on the sea that some men were being tossed around. When they cried out to the Lord, "He brought them out of their distresses. He caused the storm to be still" (vv. 28–29 NASB). God does not always answer our prayers the way we think He should. And there are times we feel God does not answer our prayers because it is not the outcome we desire.

Sometimes, God says "no," but we do not see a definite current answer, so we feel He does not answer our prayers. Sometimes God is silent, and we think He is not there. If God is silent, it does not mean He is not there; He may be asking us to be patient and wait upon the Lord. The difference is that God sees the future; we do not. Sometimes things happen for the best, even though we do not see it in the present. Further along those lines, sometimes God allows adverse events to happen to get our attention. Therefore, we need to fix our eyes on the Lord—in the good and bad times.

> Yet those who wait for the LORD
> Will gain new strength;
> They will mount up *with* wings like eagles,
> They will run and not get tired,
> They will walk and not become weary.
> (Isaiah 40:31 NASB)

Another point to consider is that bad things happen to good people because our world is in darkness and full of sin. An essential item to remember is that we may not receive our blessings here on earth. We will receive our rewards in heaven—Earth is temporary, but heaven is eternal.

Therefore, because of my own decisions and mistakes, I would never judge anyone in any way, shape, or form, and that is why I like to consider things as a journey taken together. I want to share with you a spiritually life-saving statement: You can make a U-Turn for God, and He will accept you right where you are in your life! When we turn to God, we become new creatures in Christ; thus, we are the clay, and our Lord is the potter, and we become the work of His hand (Isaiah 64:8).

We all make mistakes, or as some may say, *missed the mark.* Our all-knowing God knows this about us, and He offers us a way out. God gives us a chance to change our behavior and be redeemed (1 John 1:9, John 3:16, Colossians 1:13–14).

DeStefano, through his book, *hell (a guide),* relates to us the following.

> Listen, you're always going to experience setbacks and falls and lapses in the spiritual life.[13]
>
> But no matter what you do, as long as you sincerely desire to turn back to God, you can be forgiven. As the Bible says, "Though your sins are like scarlet, they shall be as white as snow."[14]
> Taken from Isaiah 1:18 NIV

---

[13] Anthony DeStefano, *hell (a guide),* (Nashville: Nelson Books, 2020), 184.

[14] DeStefano, *hell,* 184.

For edification, I would like to add that the words scarlet and crimson also refer to the Lamb's blood (Revelation 7:14 NIV) of Jesus Christ, not just a term for our sins. Thus, His crimson blood washes away our scarlet sins and makes us white as snow!

> **The** "Lamb of God" is described for us in Paul Kent's book, *Who Is Jesus?*

> Jesus was the one perfect sacrifice for human sin.[15] We all have a problem—sin—and we can all "behold" the solution: Jesus, the Lamb of God. His sacrifice covers everyone who turns to Him in humble faith.[16]

> For I know the plans I have for you, declares the Lord, plans for welfare and not for evil, to give you a future and a hope. (Jeremiah 29:11 ESV)

> In him was life, and the life was the light of men. (John 1:4 ESV)

> There is a ray of hope, for Jesus is the "light of the world" (John 8:12 NIV).

> He has delivered us from the domain of darkness and transferred us to the kingdom of his beloved Son, in whom we have redemption, the forgiveness of sins. (Colossians 1:13–14 ESV)

---

[15] Paul Kent, *Who Is Jesus?* (Uhrichsville: Barbour Publishing, Inc., 2020), 52.
[16] Ibid., 53.

Another spiritual factor to remember is that even though we have been forgiven of our sins, we are not released from those sins' consequences. Yet, unbelievers can have a change of heart and call upon the Lord! Therefore, one essential benefit believers have is they have the Lord guiding them through their learning lessons—unbelievers do not.

I sincerely hope that the above scripture and quotations from others offered you a sense of peace, comfort, and perhaps some joy to help you overcome or assist you in your time of suffering. My main message throughout this book is that God does love you. The primary question is, are you going to accept His love and return it?

Introduction to the Three Views

After reading various online articles regarding hell over four years ago (mid-2017), I started researching conditionalism, universalism, and traditionalism. I was curious because, until then, I had not heard of those exact terms. I had always thought all evangelical Christians believed that the lake of fire was eternal for unbelievers, so it was a learning curve for me during that time.

From my research, I have discovered some interesting data regarding the three views. Some Christians believe that all these views are evangelical and scriptural; I'm afraid I disagree with that, and I will debate the concept in Chapter 1. This book is not a comprehensive, comparative study about these three views; however, I have dedicated Chapter 1 to describing and summarizing them. Two of these views—conditionalism and traditionalism—have been detailed in *Two Views of Hell* by Edward William Fudge and Robert A. Peterson (2000).

Briefly stated, the three central beliefs regarding the fate of unbelievers in the lake of fire are these.

- Traditionalism: eternal punishment in the eternal fire.
- Conditionalism: complete annihilation; body and soul cease to exist.
- Universalism: temporary; eventually, everyone will be saved.

While researching these views, I found some information about a fourth view: eternal separation. I will not summarize or compare this view in Chapter 1, but I wanted to be fair-minded and offer a definition. "Eternal separation is a softer and increasingly popular view where the unbeliever is eternally separated from God—in this view the fire is treated as a *metaphor.*"[17] In eternal separation and traditionalism, Loewen describes, "in either of these, the unbeliever will never die or be freed from this state of punishment."[18] Eternal separation is like the traditionalist viewpoint in that both existences are infinite, yet with eternal separation, the fire is symbolic, not eternal.

As I mentioned in my Background, in the article I first read regarding Conditionalism, the author Moritz also stated, "that you have to look at the entire Bible and what it says, and you need to consider the nature and character of God."[19] I wholeheartedly agree with the author's statement, and we will

____

[17] Chris Loewen, *A case for Conditionalism*, rethinkinghell.com, May 30, 2018.

[18] Ibid.

[19] Moritz, *Hell.*

discover throughout the following chapters just how important that statement is.

Intellectually we all know the Bible cannot teach three views of hell, or the Bible would be a work of fiction. So instead, the Bible teaches one view of the lake of fire: making two views unscriptural. We will review this theory in Chapter 1.

Wrapping Up the Introduction

I have not put a title on myself as a traditionalist when it comes to my spiritual beliefs. I believe in the evangelical way, but I know people usually equate being evangelical with being traditional. Yet, those who believe in the other views consider themselves evangelical.

I respectfully feel that we are either Christian or not. We choose to believe in the Word of God or not. I do not think that Christianity is a religion—It is a faith in Jesus Christ. Religion seems to be full of rules and regulations. However, Christianity does have two essential commandments (Mark 12:28–31 NASB): love the Lord your God with all your heart (v. 30a) and love your neighbor as yourself (v. 31). To show that we love God, we live in submission to His will and are obedient to His commandments (John 14:15). Therefore, we do not need rules and regulations to conduct our lives based on those two commandments.

As an encouragement, the Bible tells us, "If anyone serves me, he must follow me; and where I am, there will my servant be also; if anyone serves Me, the Father will honor him" (John 12:26 NASB).

It is vital for those who profess to be Christians to remember that we are evangelists by spreading the Word of God, the gospel of Jesus Christ, to an unbelieving world.

Let us now travel together to study and review what those three views are all about.

PART TWO

A Biblical Overview of God's Attributes and His Divine Wrath

CHAPTER 1
Three Views of The Lake of Fire

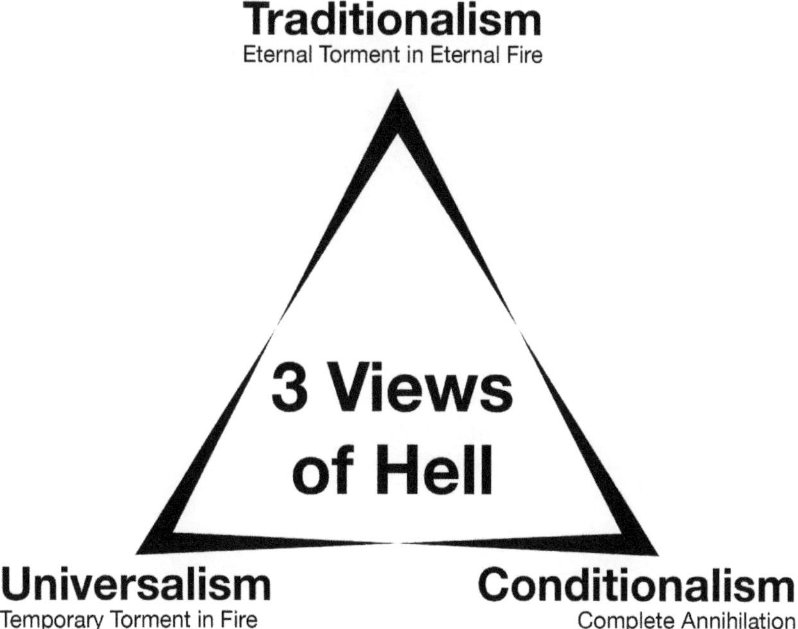

Definitions and Summaries

Comparing the Views

CHAPTER 1

The Three Views of the Lake of Fire

An Overview

In my introduction, I listed three main viewpoints and a brief explanation. This book is not a detailed comparison of the three views, but I felt it was necessary to dive deeper into those three perspectives.

I will start with the two popular views, and people seem to be more open to these philosophies: conditionalism and universalism. I will then discuss traditionalism; this view is the least accepted, and people turn from it.

Definitions and Summaries

Conditionalism

Conditionalism by a Conditionalist

Loewen, in his article *The Case for Conditionalism*, defines this view as

[Briefly] Conditionalism is the view that we are not all eternal or immortal beings, unlike God. Eternal life and immortality is "conditional" upon faith in Jesus Christ, and are given as a good gift, not a curse. When the condition of salvation is not met, hell is a place of complete destruction and annihilation. In this view, the unbeliever eventually perishes and ceases to be.[20]

Terminal Punishment (Similar to Conditionalism).

Stackhouse, contributing author of *Four Views On Hell*, describes this view as

Unbelievers will indeed be punished in hell, yet that punishment will consist of death and destruction. Unbelievers will *not* live forever in a state of conscious torment, for their life will be terminated after judgment day.[21]

Summary

My understanding is that the conditionalism belief is widespread and increasing among evangelicals. I am alarmed, for the Bible does not teach this view. Evangelicals believe in conditionalism, but that does not make conditionalism or other nonbiblical viewpoints evangelical; that philosophy is a slippery slope.

---

[20] Loewen, *Conditionalism.*

[21] Preston Sprinkle, Denny Burk, John Stackhouse Jr., Robin Perry, and Jerry Walls, *Four Views On Hell* (Grand Rapids: Zondervan, 2016), 13.

Conditionalism is comforting when you first look at it. Those who do not accept Jesus Christ as their personal Savior, those who are unsaved sinners or unbelievers, will just die in the lake of fire—complete annihilation. No pain, no suffering, no long-term discomfort, and no consequences. Sounds good, doesn't it? But is it the truth?

How is death (ceasing to exist) punishment? Death is not punishment. Yes, it is true our bodies die, and that is final—until the resurrection (Daniel 12:2; John 5:29; 1 Corinthians 15). Yet our souls are eternal. Therefore, if unbelievers cease to exist, there are no consequences—eternal or otherwise.

I have heard on the Christian radio many times the following example of why a loving God would send people to the lake of fire for eternal punishment: A surgeon needs to use wrath against cancer. He needs to cut out the tumor from the rest of the body so it can remain good. God is good, not evil. God needs to cut the cancer of sin out of humankind. I am not saying that those with cancer have sinned; I am explaining what God needs to do.

The other matter we need to discuss is Satan's fate. Do Satan and his demons get off the hook with mere death? No consequences for them, either? The Bible is clear regarding their fate (Revelation 19:20, 20:10). Are conditionalists stating that there are no consequences for sin for anyone? Death holds no consequences, so how is that punishment?

Death, Cessation of Life (body and soul), is not Eternal Punishment

Let me explain. The theory of ceasing to exist has no aftermath. Yes, you are dead, but you have no after-thoughts, grief, regret, or shame.

When we were young, we were punished when we did wrong. Punish means "to inflict pain or any evil on, as a penalty; to chastise, to hurt."[22] Our parents did not annihilate us, and no, they did not punish us for eternity either. We need to remind ourselves that our parents are not the Almighty God who administers Divine Wrath. While we were being disciplined, we were thinking about things—mental anguish? Isn't that what punishment is all about—learning from our mistakes or analyzing what we did wrong?

One could also ask, *what sense does eternal punishment make*? Even if those in the lake of fire learn something or have regrets, there is no retribution or reconciliation—their fate is final, and thus, eternal conscious torment. The torment is: You will be aware you are separated from God, knowing of your sin, while in an environment of total darkness and never consumed by the unquenchable fire—for eternity!

Many may question: Why is there eternal punishment? Why would God create such a place? What is the purpose?

Simply stated, we are sinners, yet there is nothing simple about sin—we are detestable, wicked, evil, and defiled. We cannot come before God in that state no matter how much He loves us (John 14:6; Revelation 21:27). Sin is a severe issue; even though some may not think they are sinners, some may think *I'm a good person.* Some may also think, *why would I be punished for eternity for just telling a white lie?* If a person believes that the only sin they have committed is a white lie, they are genuinely deceiving themselves. However, even a white lie is evil before God—"For all have sinned" (Romans

---

[22] "Punish" *New Roget's Thesaurus and Webster's Dictionary* (Miami: Paradise Press, Inc., 1994), 150.

3:23). I will be discussing the seriousness and magnitude of sin later in this book.

Let's go back to the Garden of Eden. God walked with Adam and Eve daily (Genesis 3:8 KJV) until Adam and Eve sinned by disobeying God by eating the forbidden fruit. From that moment on, the fellowship between God and man was broken—until Jesus. Jesus bridges the gap of separation, but only if we believe in Him.

The punishment for disobeying God by eating the forbidden fruit was death. At that moment, they did not die a physical death; they died a spiritual death. "For since by a man death *came*, by a man also *came* the resurrection of the dead. For as in Adam all die, so also in Christ all will be made alive" (1 Corinthians 15:21–22 NASB). Adam and Eve lived for hundreds of years. Adam lived for 930 years (Genesis 5:5), but Eve's lifespan is not definite. Thus, we are all spiritually dead until we choose Jesus Christ as we live a physical life on earth. Whether we are redeemed or not, we live a physical life here on earth until our physical death. Condemnation is eternal until we are cleansed from all unrighteousness (1 John 1:9) through salvation in Jesus Christ as our personal Savior—in other words, "whosoever believeth" (John 3:16 KJV). Through the decision of believing in Jesus, we will "also in Christ all will be made alive" (1 Corinthians 15:22 NASB).

Some may feel that death is eternal punishment. An excellent example is explained by Moritz as follows, "that in my view, it is an 'eternal punishment' because it is eternal in its consequences (not duration). i.e., there's no coming back from it."[23] One might also say that death is a punishment versus not

---

[23] Jeremy Moritz, email dialogue, October 29, 2020.

going to heaven. Still, we need to look at why people do not go to heaven—They do not receive the reward of eternal life in heaven because they rejected God (the unpardonable sin, Matthew 12:31–32). Another way of defining it: "For all have sinned" (Romans 3:23 KJV). "For the wages of sin is death," as described in the Bible (Romans 6:23 KJV). Is your name in the Book of Life? (Revelation 20:15) Again, death is spiritual death, not the cessation of body and soul.

Others believe that eternal punishment is annihilation; once you die, you are eternally dead and never enter heaven. This concept sounds good, but is it the truth? Matthew 25:31–46 makes it clear who goes to heaven and who goes to the lake of fire, and 2 Thessalonians 1:8–9 is clear regarding the environment of the lake of fire. So, neither passage says complete annihilation.

In Revelation 22:12–14 (NIV), Jesus is telling us that He is the "Alpha and Omega;" "blessed are those who have the right to the tree of life (v 14).

However, in Revelation 22:15 (NIV), Jesus tells us, "outside are the dogs, those who practice magic arts, the sexually immoral, the murderers, the idolaters and everyone who loves and practices falsehood." If unbelievers were merely dead, Jesus would not have told us this.

To further prove that the lake of fire is not complete annihilation, I suggest we review Matthew 13:41–42 (NASB), "The Son of Man will send forth His angels, and they will gather out of His kingdom all stumbling blocks, and those who commit lawlessness, and they will throw them into the furnace of fire; in that place there will be weeping and gnashing of teeth." In some translations, "weeping" is replaced with "wailing" (KJV). Therefore, if there is complete annihilation (cessation of life), one would be silent. However, in the above verse, it does not sound like silence. In other words, if you are dead, you are dead—no aftermath. Moreover, when you are *just* dead, you will not suffer or think that you are not in heaven. So I question how is just being dead eternal punishment according to scripture (Matthew 25:46) and the definition of the word *punish*?

Additionally, if the unbeliever is *just* dead, they will not know they are dead eternally—because they are dead—no thought process! Further, the unbeliever will not be aware they are "punished eternally" because they are forever dead—no after-thoughts. Again, how is death a punishment? The conditionalists death means a pure death, in which there is no physical or mental pain or anguish of any kind; therefore, the dead do not know they are dead or punished by death. It seems to me that unsaved sinners can sin all their lives and then be blessed with just mere death, no punishment of any kind for their sins. Moreover, the dead will not know they did not go to heaven as a punishment because they died. In this case, how is death a penalty?

We need to consider a second important position that sin does not go away, even when one is in the "lake of fire." Those in the lake of fire do not become "new creatures"[24] or suddenly become saved. On the contrary, the punishment for sin is horrific and eternal. "They do not in hell love the Lord their God with heart, mind, soul, and strength."[25]

The above representation helps us also understand that the universalist perspective of reconciling with God after death is impossible.

----

[24] Russell Moore, *Why Is Hell Eternal*? http://www.christianity.com/wiki/heaven-and-hell/why-is-hell-eternal.html. Retrieved on March 19, 2020.

[25] Ibid.

There is only one lake of fire, not two: There is no eternal lake of fire for *just* Satan, etc., and then another is complete annihilation for all others (Revelation 20:10). "Revelation 20:10 also paints a picture of hell being a place where people 'will be tormented day and night.' If we were simply destroyed, we would not see this type of language."[26] Additional scripture confirms there is one lake of fire.

> Then death and Hades were thrown into the lake of fire. This is the second death, the lake of fire. And if anyone's name was not found written in the book of life, he was thrown into the lake of fire. (Revelation 20:14–15 NASB)

If you will note, the scripture does not state "lakes of fire," it says, "lake of fire."

The Lake of Fire Is the Lake of Fire

I am not suggesting that conditionalists believe there are two lakes of fire; however, do they believe that Satan, the beast, and the false prophet get off the hook with mere death?

I prefer what Jesus said about Judgment Day in Matthew.

> Then He will also say to those on His left, Depart from Me, accursed people, into the eternal fire which has been prepared for the devil and his angels. (Matthew 25:41 NASB)

---

[26] Clinton E. Arnold and Jeff Arnold, *Short Answers to BIG Questions about God, the Bible & Christianity* (Michigan: Baker Books, 2015), 136.

These will go away into eternal punishment, but the righteous into eternal life. (Matthew 25:46 NASB)

Let us think about what Jesus said above.

- Was this a parable?
- Was this a metaphor?
- Was Jesus talking out of both sides of His mouth?
- Was Jesus not stating the truth?
- Was He making stuff up?

Jesus did not say that only heaven was eternal. Jesus never said "eternal life" in the lake of fire; He said, "eternal punishment."

Additional scriptures such as in Daniel 12:2 and John 5:29 correspond with this—that we are raised for "everlasting life" or "everlasting contempt" (NASB), and respectively, a "resurrection of life" or "resurrection of judgment" (NASB). The Word of God does not state or infer complete annihilation or ceasing to exist. It is clear; the Word of God teaches the opposite.

Part of the conditionalists definition is that eternal life is not meant as a curse. Scripture is clear. In Matthew 25:41 (NASB), God used the words "accursed people" and said they would be going into the eternal fire.

Revelation 14:11 says, "The smoke of their torment goes up forever and ever." Scripture seems to be communicating to us in every possible way that life after death is eternal, whether that be with

God or apart from God.[27] Scripture noted is taken from the ESV Bible.

Conditionalists strongly believe that salvation is a gift of God through belief in Jesus Christ as our Savior. Furthermore, the gift of salvation gives believers eternal life in heaven, whereas unbelievers will be annihilated in the lake of fire.

The traditionalist view believes fundamentally the same regarding believers, except that traditionalists believe in eternal punishment in the lake of fire, not just death for the unbelievers. Therefore, since death is not punishment or retribution for one's sins, the unbelievers' souls will be in an eternal state of judgment in the eternal fire.

Universalism

Definition of Universalism

> Christian Universalism is a school of Christian theology focused around the doctrine universal reconciliation—the view that all human beings will ultimately be "saved" and restored to a right relationship to God.[28]

After reading this definition, I noticed the following further down on the Wikipedia page.

> Christians from a diversity of denominations and traditions believe in the tenets of Christian

---

[27] Arnold, *Short Answers to BIG* Questions, 136.

[28] "Christian Universalism," Wikipedia.

universalism, such as the reality of an afterlife without the possibility of eternal punishment in hell.[29]

A Definition of Universalism by a Conditionalist

Loewen describes this viewpoint as follows.

Universalism is the view of hell as a place of burning which is refining and purifying with the ultimate purpose that all will eventually come to a place of repentance and restoration with God and then enter Heaven. The length of time for this purified repentance will vary for each unbeliever, but God's love, according to Universalists, is powerful enough to bring all to repentance and restoration. In other words, hell will eventually empty itself and cease to be.[30]

A Definition of Universalism by a Universalist

DeRose, author of the article *Universalism and the Bible: The Really Good News*, describes this view as:

Universalism refers to the position that eventually all human beings will be saved and will enjoy everlasting life with Christ. This is compatible with the view that God will punish many people after death, and many Universalists accept that there will be divine retribution, although some

---

[29] "Christian Universalism," Wikipedia.

[30] Loewen, *Conditionalism*.

may not. What universalism does commit one to is that such punishment won't last forever.[31]

Ultimate Reconciliation

The definition of Christian universalism, also known as ultimate reconciliation, is offered by contributing author Parry of *Four Views On Hell*. Parry defines this idea as follows.

> …that only one road leads to heaven (or the new creation): the way of Christ. Yet all creation, through the atoning work of Christ, will ultimately be reconciled to its Creator. While some Christians embrace universalism out of sentiment and an unwillingness to believe in a God who could send people to hell …[32] that the future judgment will be followed by reconciliation.[33]

Summary

After reading and pondering the above definitions, I had some concerns regarding this perspective. I found this philosophy difficult to comprehend spiritually. I love to read what Jesus said. He never explained in His Word that there was a purification process or that a person could reconcile with God after death. In the following summation, I will document with scripture that God's Word does not support this philosophy.

We need to go back to Matthew 25:31–46. I do not know

---

[31] Keith DeRose, "Universalism and the Bible." Retrieved on April 9, 2020, from http://campuspress.yale.edu/keithderose/1129–2/.

[32] Sprinkle, *Four Views On Hell*, 13–14.

[33] Ibid., 14.

how much clearer Jesus needed to make it. Jesus did not say complete annihilation, nor did He state that there was a purification process after death for unbelievers, and then they were able to enter heaven.

Daniel 12:2 and John 5:29 clearly state "eternal" for two different destinations for one's body and soul. There is nothing in these verses that discusses complete annihilation or a purification process. Yes, because humanity fell into sin in the Garden of Eden, we go from dust to dust (Genesis 3:19), but that dust will rise!

We need to count on the scriptures to tell us the truth, and our Bible does not lie or contradict itself. Believers and unbelievers will be resurrected (the dust will rise) and receive new immortal bodies (1 Corinthians 15, especially vv. 52–57); however, the unbeliever will have a different fate. We will be in one of two eternal places—believers eternally in heaven with our Lord and unbelievers forever in the lake of fire without God.

> The Son of Man will send forth His angels, and they will gather out of His kingdom all stumbling blocks, and those who commit lawlessness, and they will throw them into the furnace of fire; in that place there will be weeping and gnashing of teeth. (Matthew 13:41–42 NASB)

Scripture speaks loud and clear. After reading God's Word, you will understand that there is no purification process. The above scripture also lets us know that the lake of fire is not complete annihilation, as the conditionalists believe.

Luke 16:19–31, regarding the rich man and Lazarus, is an essential passage in several ways. First, it has a much deeper message than the rich man wanting a drop of water on his tongue, yet this is crucial in explaining that he was thirsty and in agony because of where he was. Second, this passage is vital in explaining some of our afterlife questions. In Chapter 3, I briefly summarize this passage, and in Chapter 5, I detail its deeper meaning.

If the rich man were undergoing a purification process, why did he ask Abraham if Lazarus could warn his five brothers? If there was indeed a purification process, why did his brothers need to receive a warning? His brothers would only need to obtain an alert if there was no hope of getting out of the lake of fire. Abraham not only turned down the rich man's request but told him, "They have Moses and the prophets; let them hear them" (Luke 16:29 NASB).

To further explain the above concept, I suggest the following.

> Then the rich man said, "No, father Abraham, but if someone goes to them from the dead, they will repent! But he said to him, If they do not listen to Moses and the prophets, they will not be persuaded even if someone rises from the dead." (Luke16: 30–31 NASB)

The above documentation informs us that once we die as an unbeliever, there is no way of escaping the eternal punishment of the lake of fire.

> Let's examine just one of the passages the universalists use.[34]

---

[34] DeRose, "Universalism."

> For in him all the fullness of God was pleased to dwell, and through him to reconcile to himself all things, whether on earth or in heaven, making peace by the blood of his cross. (Colossians 1:19–20 ESV)

First, the words "to reconcile to himself all things" do not mean a purification process in the lake of fire to reconcile with God. Throughout the Bible, passages describe that He will be over all, all things were created by Him and through Him (John 1:1–5), and the government will rest on His shoulders (Isaiah 9:6 NASB). So, when you join all the scripture, it does not describe reconciliation from eternal punishment.

Further, those who believe in this viewpoint emphasized the word *all*. It is true what scripture says. Other passages tell us that Jesus died for all (Romans 6:10; 2 Corinthians 5:14–15). Yes, indeed, He died for all; the scriptures do not lie. However, it does not negate other passages in the Bible. When we correlate those passages, we learn some interesting facts. Let us examine a familiar verse.

> If we confess our sins, He is faithful and just to forgive us our sins and to cleanse us from all unrighteousness. (1 John 1:9 KJV)

The operative word is *if.* The entire world is condemned from birth since its original sin. To be removed from that status, we need to ask forgiveness of our sins—of our own free will. Christ shed His precious blood and died on the cross for all, but that does not mean that all are automatically saved. There is no *umbrella* or *blanket*, automatic saving process.

Let us also examine another well-known verse, John 3:16 (KJV).

> For God so loved the world, that he gave his only begotten Son, that whosoever believeth in him should not perish, but have everlasting life.

The operative word is *believeth*. This verse tells us that "whosoever believeth" means all individuals making independent decisions choose to believe or not believe—meaning further, we need to choose to believe in Jesus Christ personally. It is only through redemption in Christ and Christ alone that we are saved. Again, it is not an automatic saving system to all, yet all who decide to follow Jesus are indeed saved. Halleluiah! Amen!

We will now probe into a verse that backs up John 3:16. I think it is essential we examine two translations to clarify their meaning.

> The Lord is not slack concerning *His* promise, as some count slackness, but is longsuffering toward us, not willing that any should perish but that all should come to repentance. (2 Peter 3:9 NKJV)

> The Lord isn't really being slow about his promise, as some people think. No, he is being patient for your sake. He does not want anyone to be destroyed, but wants everyone to repent. (2 Peter 3:9 NLT)

Both versions speak of the Lord's patience with us. One may ask, *How is the Lord patient?* Well, the rapture has not happened yet. The world is not yet destroyed. Thus, if you are reading this, you are still alive and can decide to repent.

Further, both translations tell us the Lord does not want us to perish (NKJV) or be destroyed (NLT). Simply stated, the words perish and destroyed mean eternal punishment or everlasting judgment. Finally, each rendition tells us that the Lord wants us to come to repentance (NKJV) and everyone to repent (NLT). Therefore, each person needs to make an independent decision to repent.

An additional scripture that backs up John 3:16 is John 14:6, "Jesus saith unto him, I am the way, the truth, and the life: no man cometh unto the Father, but by me" (KJV). It is evident in this passage that the only way to God the Father is through Jesus Christ, "whosoever believeth," so we will not perish. These words do not add up to a purification process to reconcile with God after death. We need to go through Jesus Christ so we will not perish. Perish does not mean we enter a fiery lake to reconcile with God and ultimately enter heaven; perish in this sense is eternal punishment in the eternal fire. That is why Jesus died on the cross to save us from that eternal peril—if we only believe—whosoever believeth.

Another verse we need to consider, and I believe imperative, will prove that we need to make our spiritual decision to follow Christ before we die.

> And as it is appointed unto men once to die, but after this the judgment. (Hebrews 9:27 KJV)

"Once to die" means a person's physical death. Those who

die are judged. Unsaved sinners (unbelievers) will go before God to be condemned for their sins (Matthew 13:42; Revelation 20:15); however, saved sinners (believers) will go before Jesus to have their works judged by fire.

Our "works" do not get us into heaven "so that no one can boast" (see Ephesians 2:8–10 NIV), yet we will have our works judged by fire for worthiness (1 Corinthians 3:10–15; 1 Peter 1:7). Believers will receive crowns of glory for their "works" and faith (2 Timothy 4:8; James 1:12; 1 Peter 5:4; Revelation 2:10, 3:11), and those crowns of glory will last forever (1 Corinthians 9:15). We will all be standing before God for judgment. Believers will be judged for their works, and the unbelievers will be judged for their sins. And our Father judges with impartiality "according to each one's deeds" (1 Peter 1:17 ESV).

Additionally, Colossians 1:19–20 (ESV) says, "on earth or in heaven,"; it does not speak of "the lower regions of the earth, Hades or the lake of fire." Therefore, persons who are in these regions are not included in "the *all.*" All does mean all, and I do not debate that. I have shown scripture that assists us in understanding what the Word of God is telling us. We should not take scripture out of context; we must look at other passages to know the meaning and carefully consider the operative words.

Let's go back in time to the crucifixion of Jesus and the two thieves. There is a specific dialogue in Luke 23:39–43 that we need to consider if there is a purification process for unbelievers after their physical death or not. In the following brief study, I will be using words from the NASB version.

One of the thieves starts the conversation off by "hurling abuse" at Jesus, "saying, Are you not the Christ? Save yourself and save us" (v 39). The other thief rebukes his fellow thief saying, "Do you not even fear God?" (v 40), and shares that they are receiving "what we deserve, but this man has done nothing wrong" (v 41). Finally, the now repentant thief says, "Jesus, remember me when You come into Your kingdom!" (v 42). Now comes the beautiful words from Jesus to the penitent thief, "Truly I say to you, today you will be with me in paradise" (v.43).

Let's now dive a little deeper. First, the unrepentant thief rebuked Jesus; he was not trying to reconcile with Him; however, he was not dead yet. Perhaps unredeemed persons do not learn of this purification process until they are dead and judged by God. If you also notice, Jesus did not offer any hope to the unrepentant thief either. Why? If there were a purification process after death, this would have been the perfect time for Jesus to let the guy know. Secondly, Jesus assured the repentant thief the hope of paradise, yet He did not offer that same hope or any hope to the unrepentant thief. Why? Because it would conflict with words that Jesus said during His ministry (Matthew 25:31–46 NASB), "Depart from Me, you accursed people, into the eternal fire" (v 41), and "These will go away into eternal punishment" (v 46). Further, those whose names are not written in the book of life were thrown into the lake of fire (Revelation 20:15).

Moreover, John the Baptist, Jesus, and all His disciples, including Apostle Paul, would be sharing a reconciliation process to reconcile with God after death throughout all their ministries and travels, but they do not preach that philosophy. Scripture is clear on eternal punishment in the eternal fire and is not hidden from us. I know the Bible includes some mysteries, yet I do not believe that we need to hunt and decipher the scriptures to find proof of reconciliation with God after death. If there were such a process, it would be apparent in the Scriptures, as clear as "eternal fire" and eternal punishment." Next, we will look at additional scriptures that do not support reconciliation with God after death.

The other issue I see with a purification process is that through scriptures, the environment of the lake of fire is not conducive to purification or reconciling with God. The following passage is an evident representation of the lake of fire.

> In flaming fire, inflicting vengeance on those who do not know God and on those who do not obey the gospel of our Lord Jesus. They will suffer the punishment of eternal destruction, away from the presence of the Lord and from the glory of his might. (2 Thessalonians 1:8–9 ESV)

How can a purification process—to reconcile with God—happen in an environment with no God for eternity? The above verse cites no purification process. Further, there is no reference to any reconciliation with God. The inhabitants of the lake of fire are away from God and away from His glory—this means God's love is not present in the lake of fire.

Moreover, we need to consider the following—simply put, "Sin is more serious than we realize, and sin does not disappear."[35]

---

[35] Moore, *Why Is Hell Eternal?* Retrieved from Christianity.com.

They do not in hell love the Lord their God with heart, mind, soul, and strength.[36]

I also have a question about Satan, his demons, the beast, and the false prophet. According to scripture, they will all be thrown into the lake of fire, and the Bible emphasizes the torment is for eternity (see above and Chapter 3). However, according to one definition of universalism, eventually, everyone will go to heaven, and then "hell will empty itself and cease to be." Additionally, another definition refers specifically to human beings. There is nothing in the Universalist's definitions regarding Satan's fate. Does this mean that Satan and his demons will be purified and go back to heaven? Does it also suggest that the beast, and the false prophet will eventually be reconciled with God and get into heaven as well?

Satan and his angels, now demons, were thrown out of heaven.

> And the great dragon was cast out, that old serpent, called the Devil, and Satan, which deceiveth the whole world: he was cast out into the earth, and his angels were cast out with him. (Revelation 12:9 KJV)

Jesus is speaking:

> And He said to them, I watched Satan fall from heaven like lightning. (Luke 10:18 NASB)

There is only one lake of fire.

---

[36] Moore, *Why Is Hell Eternal?* Retrieved from Christianity.com.

A Concept for Consideration

Let us briefly discuss atheists and others who have denied God. Simply stated, an atheist does not believe in the existence of any deities. When atheists and others who deny God die, will they automatically go through a purification process to reconcile with God and go to heaven no matter how they believed? They have refused and rejected God, and they still go to heaven? Why would a person who does not love God and has rejected Him want to be with Him for eternity? Are we robots or puppets with no choice? What about the consequences of sin?

I understand the universalist premise—God's love for them will eventually win them over in the purification process. If God's love for them did not win them over while they were alive, I highly doubt God's love will win them when they are dead, especially when the lake of fire is absent of God as I have previously described; scripture supports this (2 Thessalonians 1:8–9). How can a person reconcile with God if God is not there? It takes a relationship with God to reconcile with Him. Our God is a living God; therefore, we must be alive to reconcile with Him. (Hebrews 9:27)

The universalist premise would lead some to believe there is a postmortem opportunity for salvation, giving people a chance to change their minds about God after death. This concept is discussed and answered in Chapter 5.

It appears to me that the universalist belief is that people can sin and do whatever they want, including denying and rejecting God. Yet, they get to go to heaven anyway with no shame, regrets, or guilt for what they have done, nor do they have to ask God for forgiveness (1 John 1:9). Instead, the belief is that because God loves them so much, they will be reconciled with Him in the fiery lake, which is considered refining and purifying. Therefore, I ask this question: Whether they believe in God or not?

To probe further, I would like to discuss two other important points. First, a little earlier, I was discussing the crucifixion of Jesus. The unrepentant thief rebuked Jesus by saying, "Save yourself and save us" (v 39). For humanity to be saved, Jesus needed to die and be raised from the dead; therefore, if Jesus did as the thief requested, everyone would remain condemned. Thus, there would be no available salvation for humankind. The point of this dialogue is Jesus needed to die to save us; therefore, we need to believe in Jesus before our death to be raised as new creatures in Christ.

The second point of this dialogue is that the concept of reconciling with God after death negates scripture, such as John 14:6, "Jesus saith unto him, I am the way, the truth, and the life: no man cometh unto the Father, but by me" (KJV). We are saved only through Jesus Christ by freely accepting the salvation offered to us, "whosoever believeth shall not perish, but have everlasting life" (John 3:16 KJV). Perish does not mean a final death or temporary punishment to reconcile with God after death; it means eternal punishment as a soul's final destination in eternal fire.

Conditionalism is comparable to the degree that unbelievers can sin and reject God, as stated above, yet there are no consequences—only death. The Bible does not teach either philosophy. I do not believe that Jesus came down from heaven to die on the cross if only death or a purification process were for unbelievers upon their death.

Spiritually speaking, I feel that this shows a diminished perception of what Jesus did on the cross. Jesus said, "eternal punishment," and He wanted to save us from it. He did not say a purification process.

Salvation is a gift from God through belief in Jesus Christ, and our reward is eternal life in heaven with Him—we cannot earn it, work for it, or after death, go through a purification process to receive it. Salvation is only through Jesus Christ as a personal decision ("whosoever believeth" John 3:16) before someone's death (Hebrews 9:27).

Traditionalism

A Definition of Traditionalism by a Conditionalist

Loewen defines this view for us as follows.

> The predominant view is traditionalism which is the perspective that we are all eternal beings who will live forever either in heaven or hell... Eternal torment is the more "traditional" view where the unbeliever is tormented in *literal* fire … the unbeliever will never die or be freed from this state of punishment.[37]

After a further Internet search, I found the following that helps describe the traditionalist belief.

---

[37] Loewen, *Conditionalism.*

Death and Afterlife

Christian anthropology has implications for belief about death and afterlife. The Christian has traditionally taught that the soul of each individual separates from the body at death, to be reunited at the resurrection.[38]

Final State

In Christian belief, both the righteous and the unrighteous will be resurrected at the last judgment. The righteous will receive incorruptible, immortal bodies (1 Corinthians 15), while the unrighteous will be sent to hell. Traditionally, Christians have believed that hell will be a place of eternal physical and psychological punishment.[39]

A Definition of Traditionalism by a Traditionalist

Burk, one of the contributing authors of *Four Views On Hell*, explains traditionalism as follows.

Hell is a place where the wicked will experience everlasting conscious torment.[40]

---

[38] "Christian Anthropology," Wikipedia.

[39] Ibid.

[40] Sprinkle, *Four Views On Hell*, 13.

> The traditional view of hell makes the most sense
> of what the Bible says about the character of God
> and the magnitude of sin.[41]

Summary

I grew up with the traditional view of the lake of fire. I have always thought that is what all Christians believed. But, as I discussed in the introduction, I never really viewed myself as a traditionalist, just an evangelical Christian.

As I studied all three views, I learned that traditionalism is the least popular belief and that more evangelical Christians are turning to one of the other viewpoints. Conditionalism seems to be gaining popularity over universalism. Perhaps people prefer to believe that unbelievers will just die instead of going through a fiery purification process.

It may be challenging for us to grasp in our minds such a horrifying thought of eternal existence of eternal torment in the unquenchable fire for unbelievers upon their death, but the scriptures are clear.

In the following four chapters and the conclusion, I have laid out a complete description and biblical passages to fully support the fact that the lake of fire is a final place for unbelievers. It is a place of eternal, conscious torment that includes physical pain "where THEIR WORM DOES NOT DIE, AND THE FIRE IS NOT EXTINGUISHED" (Mark 9:48 NASB), with no hope of complete annihilation or reconciliation with God. Thus, the lake of fire is a place without God. For a biblical explanation of the above, I cite the following passage:

____

[41] Ibid.

Then they will go out and look At the corpses of the people Who have rebelled against Me. For their worm will not die And their fire will not be extinguished; And they will be an abhorrence to all mankind. (Isaiah 66:24 NASB)

And as they go out, they will see the dead bodies of those who have rebelled against me. For the worms that devour them will never die, and the fire that burns them will never go out. All who pass by will view them with utter horror. (Isaiah 66:24 NLT)

- ✓ Rebelled also means Transgressed (KJV)
- ✓ Abhorrence also means loathsome (NIV), and utter horror (NLT)

Where the maggots never die and the fire never goes out. (Mark 9:48 NLT)

Traditionalism is the least popular view; it sounds harsh, and it paints God as cruel and unloving, whereas the other viewpoints have a softer approach to God's wrath. However, we need to ask, what is the truth?

God's Word speaks of His immense love for us through His sacrificial love for us when He sent His only begotten Son to take on the sins of the world. But there is a condition for salvation from the eternal lake of fire; of our own free will, we need to accept Jesus Christ as our Lord and personal Savior before our physical death.

Comparing the Views

When I contrasted all three views, I found some common threads.

- All agree that everyone who accepted Jesus Christ before their physical death will have eternal life in heaven. Universalists believe a person can enter heaven after death through a purification process to reconcile with God.
- All believe in a lake of fire; they just have a different view of what it is.
- All accept as true that their beliefs are scriptural.

Traditionalists and universalists believe that our souls are eternal, whereas conditionalists believe that not all souls are eternal—specifically, the souls of the unbelievers are not immortal. The traditionalist's view is that one's soul has one of two destinations: those who die as believers will go to eternal life in heaven, yet those who die as unbelievers will go to the eternal fire.

Universalists believe that everyone's soul will be eternally in heaven—eventually. Those who die as believers will go to heaven, and those who die as unbelievers will go through a purification process in the lake of fire and eventually go to heaven. They believe that this purification process reconciles their relationship with God; thus, after it, they can enter heaven. Our souls are eternal. A scripture passage might help with this.

> He has made everything appropriate in its time.
> He has also set eternity in their heart, without

> *the possibility that* mankind will find out the work
> which God has done from the beginning even to
> the end. (Ecclesiastes 3:11 NASB)

It seems that the conditionalists philosophy is built on human emotions, and their writings put a tremendous amount of importance on immortality. It made me feel that their focus was on immortality, not God. I completely understand the importance of eternal life, which is immortality; however, why was it offered to us through Jesus if the only other option was mere death? Jesus died to save us from a more horrific alternative—eternal punishment in the eternal fire.

Furthermore, conditionalists definition puts a condition on or limits what God can or cannot do. God's attributes include justice and judgment. Conditionalists believe in God's justice, which they think is complete annihilation in the lake of fire. However, scripture proves that punishment is eternal in the lake of fire; there is no "body and soul" cessation of life.

I also was somewhat shocked because some traditional evangelicals are turning to conditionalism and universalism. If you are grounded in the Word of God, when you read something that is not scriptural, whistles and bells should be going off as they did for me (see my Background section).

If you are grounded in the truth of the scriptures, you should know the difference. For example, some employees who work for the U.S. Treasury Department work in a room full of money; they feel it, have it in their hands, look at it, and know it is genuine. When counterfeit bills come their way, they know them; they can identify them.

The Word of God is the Word of God. No matter how you

slice it, dice it, mix it up in a blender, pour it on a cookie sheet, and bake it, the unchanging, living Word of God says what it says. Throughout this book, I have quoted what Jesus said about eternal punishment, and Jesus does not lie; His Word does not lie because He is the Word (John 1:1–18).

I am not stating or suggesting that believers in conditionalism, universalism, or other man-derived philosophies are not saved; however, their doctrine is dangerous. If a faith deters others from becoming believers in Jesus Christ, the faith is wrong.

I would like to make a point about deterring others. If people think they can live any way they want and then *will just die*, why would they want to become Christians? A Christian's life is tough, and Christians must be willing to submit to a life according to God's will. Matthew 16:24–25 (ESV) describes a Christian's life, "take up His cross and follow Me." But, unfortunately, most people want to live their lives according to their own will.

It is a known fact that people do not believe in the Bible and reject Jesus; however, Jesus is the truth, "and the truth will set you free" (John 8:32 ESV). The Christian faith is the only true faith. If a person chooses to reject the true faith, it does not mean the Bible's doctrine is wrong.

Let me explain. If a *specific* understanding keeps others from an accurate knowledge of Jesus Christ, then I believe that such a belief is wrong. Further, I think that it prevents them from living a full life rooted in God's truth.

I have heard sermons dealing with other religions and have learned that there is some truth to the different beliefs, making them dangerous. For example, a couple of prevalent religions teach that Jesus died for our sins and that we need to believe in Jesus to be saved. However, they also require people to perform works or dress a particular way to assure their salvation and be worthy of it. The Bible does not teach that—the Bible teaches the opposite. Salvation is a free gift—"whosoever believeth" (John 3:16).

The Bible teaches that we need to do works to show our obedience, not as a ticket into heaven, yet those works are proved (tested) by fire. As I stated earlier in this chapter, our works do not get us into heaven, yet we will have our works judged by fire for worthiness to receive eternal rewards (Ephesians 2:8–10; 1 Corinthians 3:13; 1 Peter 1:7). Scripture also tells us:

> For we must all appear before the judgment seat of Christ, so that each one may receive compensation for his deeds *done* through the body, in accordance with what he has done, whether good or bad. (2 Corinthians 5:10 NASB)

Analyzing the Views

I kept examining the three main viewpoints and thought that those who believe in complete annihilation quote many verses on death and take the view that those verses indicate that death is final for unbelievers. Those who believe in eternal torment quote scripture that supports eternal torment. Those who believe in a temporary lake of fire quote scripture to support their view.

Since the scripture does not lie or contradict itself, two of those views are incorrect. The Bible will not say one thing in one area about a subject and then say something opposite about it elsewhere. If that were the case, the Bible would be a work of fiction. The Bible does not teach three views of hell; it teaches one view of the lake of fire; hence, making two viewpoints contradictory to scripture.

We must consider the Bible as a whole—all-inclusive, and what it says to understand God's nature and His attributes as we ponder various passages. I disagree that scripture teaches us that the lake of fire is complete annihilation. The scriptures do not inform us that death is final for unbelievers.

Fudge brought a verse to our attention: "God is able to destroy both body and soul in hell"[42] This verse comes from Matthew 10:28. Both the NASB & KJV versions say, "able to destroy." One needs to consider the operative word *able*. It does not say "will" or "does." Yes, God "can destroy" (ESV, NIV & NLT) both soul and body, yet He does not. The endless punishment and judgment in the lake of fire cannot be compared or equated with eternal life in Heaven, yet both destinations are eternal. The lake of fire is eternal because that is what Jesus said. The Bible does not contradict itself.

Additionally, a corresponding verse tells us, "The Lord Almighty is the one you are to regard as holy, he is the one you are to fear, he is the one you are to dread" (Isaiah 8:13 NIV). "It is a dreadful thing to fall into the hands of the living God" (Hebrews 10:31 NIV). The prophet Isaiah also warned us about hell, "...their worm shall not die, their fire shall not be quenched..." (Isaiah 66:24 ESV).

I want to probe a little deeper into the scriptures surrounding "can destroy" (ESV) to fully understand the phrase's context.

---

[42] Edward William Fudge and Robert A. Peterson, *Two Views of Hell* (Downers Grove: Inter Varsity Press, 2000), 20–21.

What I tell you in the dark, say in the light, and what you hear whispered, proclaim on the housetops. And do not fear those who kill the body but cannot kill the soul. Rather fear him who can destroy both soul and body in hell. Are not two sparrows sold for a penny? And not one of them will fall to the ground apart from your Father. But even the hairs of your head are all numbered. (Matthew 10:27–30 ESV)

The above scriptures show us that our God is a God of love, is a Holy God, and is a God to dread. Our God is balanced, as we will learn in Chapter 2.

Once again, complete annihilation appears comforting. As I was reading the first online article on hell, as discussed in my Background, the author, Moritz, showed concern regarding a couple of situations that pulled on the reader's heartstrings. Such as, "Are we going to be thinking of our loved ones suffering in hell while we are in heaven?" The second one was, "What if a loved one is a POW who is being tortured daily? Wouldn't you want them just to die?" (Paraphrased from his article)[43]

I have heard the first question answered throughout my life; my father preached sermons on that subject. I will address these questions in the "In Conclusion" section.

In fairness, I did find some conditionalists did not express emotional conditions to convince the reader to believe in complete annihilation. Both types of authors based their beliefs on their interpretation of scripture, but from two different

---

[43] Moritz, *Hell.*

approaches. Even though their perspectives did not change my view, I respected their writing and found it educational.

We cannot use the emotions of our human nature to make something true that is not true. Likewise, we cannot spin the Word of God to make it say what we want it to say to prove our beliefs—the Bible is not an *a la carte* menu. The Bible warns us that we are not to change the Word of God (Deuteronomy 4:2, 12:32; Proverbs 30:6; Revelation 22:18–19). However, some may feel they are not changing the Word of God; they are interpreting the scriptures as they understand them.

I guess it is in our nature to try to change what God says, as Eve did. She was explaining to the serpent what God had said.

> We may eat fruit from the trees in the garden, but God did say, You must not eat fruit from the tree that is in the middle of the garden, and you must not touch it, or you will die. (Genesis 3:2–4 NIV)

What God did say was the following.

> And the Lord God commanded the man, "You are free to eat from any tree in the garden, but you must not eat from the tree of the knowledge of good and evil, for when you eat from it you will certainly die." (Genesis 2:16–17 NIV)

God said nothing about not touching the fruit, though it is probably an excellent idea not to touch the forbidden fruit. Humans have always been prone to want something they cannot have, which started with Eve, and therefore, when we touch what we cannot have, we usually fall into sin. God never said not to touch the forbidden fruit; He said not to eat it. Our faith in the Lord is based on what scriptures say, not on our emotions or feelings.

Chapter Summation

Regarding the three views of the lake of fire, perhaps we can all agree to disagree on unbelievers' fate at their death. Yet an essential factor remains: All of us need to know the complete truth of the scriptures, which affects our decisions to choose salvation or not. If people think there is only death for rejecting God and believe that there is no eternal punishment, they might decide not to follow Jesus. Big dilemma. I elaborate on this issue in Chapter 2. However, the most crucial factor is this: Are their names in the Book of Life? If they are, they will have access to eternal life in heaven with our Lord. We all need to be focusing on sharing the gospel of Jesus Christ with unbelievers. The true gospel of Jesus Christ is more than an entry into heaven, as I will discuss in Chapter 2.

In any of its sixty-six books from Genesis 1:1 to Revelation 22:21, there is not one verse in God's scripture stating that the lake of fire is complete annihilation or is temporary with a purification process. Instead, Jesus said it was eternal punishment in the eternal fire.

Chapter 3 describes what the Bible says about the lake of fire, who will be in it, and how long it will last. Let us now explore God's attributes and learn about His nature and character.

CHAPTER 2

A Balanced God

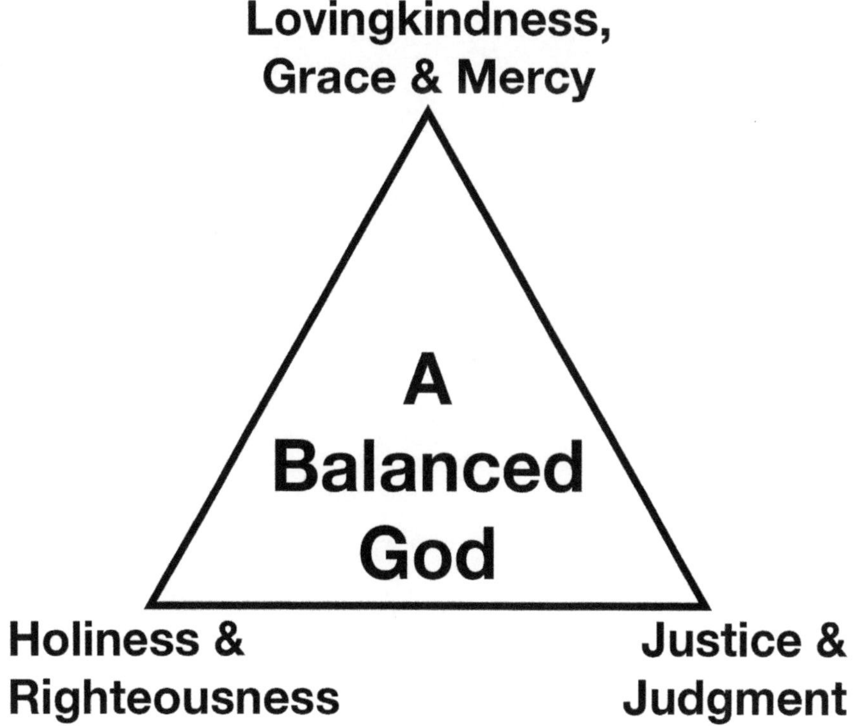

The Nature and Character of God
A Biblical Retrospect of God's Attributes

CHAPTER 2

A Balanced God

The Nature and Character of God

An Overview

This chapter will focus on God's attributes to learn about God and who He is. Above all, He is love, pure light, and pure holiness—No sin can come before Him (John 14:6; Revelation 21:27), no matter how much He loves us. God's love is His positive side, whereas there is also a negative side of God. God's negative is His anger and divine wrath of judgment of the lake of fire, which many people do not want to believe; in fact, they refute the judgment.

This chapter will also follow scriptures that lead us to prove our God is a Triune God. Additionally, we will learn about the characteristics of God that make Him balanced. When I shared my concept that God is balanced with someone, they replied, "What do you mean God is balanced?" I wanted to say, "Well, He certainly is not unbalanced." However, I tried to explain that all His attributes balance each other out; moreover, none of His characteristics can contradict each other, or He would be unbalanced. A balanced God's theology is not to be compared to a Yin-Yang or mystic type of balance. Instead, this theology helps one understand that all of God's characteristics describe Him and who He is. God does send people to the lake of fire because that is what the Bible says (Revelation 20:15). Chapter 3 discusses the biblical definitions of the lake of fire and describes the occupants. Further, Genesis 1:1, Isaiah 44:24, and Jeremiah 32:17 prove our God is balanced, for He created the heavens and the earth. All the stars, planets, and galaxies are balanced with various gravitational pulls to hold everything in its place, and only a balanced God could accomplish such a phenomenon.

> In the beginning God created the heavens and the earth.
> (Genesis 1:1 KJV)

> I, the LORD, am the maker of all things,
> Stretching out the heavens by Myself And
> spreading out the earth alone.
> (Isaiah 44:24b NASB)

> Oh, Lord GOD! Behold, You Yourself have made the heavens and the earth by Your great power and by Your outstretched arm! Nothing is too difficult for You.
> (Jeremiah 32:17 NASB)

Is God Balanced or Unbalanced?

As I was researching online to see if anyone else had written an article or book on the theology of a "Balanced God," I noticed a Sunday School lesson on the very subject; *Our*

God is Balanced. I called up the church, and to my pleasant surprise, the author, Tony Seale, answered the phone. We had a wonderful conversation and shared our beliefs on the subject. Tony permitted me to use part of his lesson in my book. The following is his perspective.

Seale shared in his lesson that God is positive and negative simultaneously. Scripture tells us that God is a consuming fire (Hebrews 12:29 KJV) and God is Love (1 John 4:8,16 KJV). "Now, it would almost seem that these two verses are contradicting one another, but in reality, God is both. He is both a consuming fire, and He is love at the same time. To be one without the other would cause God to be unbalanced."[44]

> There is a movement within the so-called modern-day Christians that focuses on God's love only, forgetting that God is both positive and negative. To take it one step further, God is not only a God of love; He also hates sin. Proverbs 6:16–19, Proverbs 8:13 lists many sins that God hates, such as lying, shedding innocent blood, and evil ways. Further, God hates these things, and as Christians, we are to hate them too (paraphrased).[45]

Seale went on to explain a deeper reason why God is balanced:

---

[44] Tony Seale, *Our God is Balanced*, Sunday School lesson 04/03/16. Retrieved on 01/10/21 (my3bc.com).

[45] Ibid.

What happens when all you preach is that God is love people start believing that God will not send anyone to hell because a loving God would not do such a thing. But we must remember that God is both Holy, Just, and Righteous, and therefore He is balanced.[46]

Seale's analysis of a balanced God is scripturally on target and is an excellent study. Tony explains simply yet thoroughly why our God is balanced. If you are interested in reading the entire lesson, see the link below in the footnotes. When you arrive at the church's website, find "search" and type in Our God is Balanced. The lesson is the first one on the list; click on it.

Along the same lines of Seale's interpretation of a balanced God, I have related that it is similar to a Triune God, God the Father, God the Son, and God the Holy Spirit. Additionally, God is balanced in these three main areas, (1) His Lovingkindness, Grace, and Mercy, (2) His Justice and Judgment, and (3) His Holiness and Righteousness. Some do not believe that our God is a Triune God; however, I will prove through scripture that He is indeed a Triune God.

I was speaking with one of my sisters, Danee, about a balanced God. She brought up another way to look at it as "God is level" (i.e., plumb). Danee related the terms, level and plumb, are similar to construction terms. She also shared that God's Word is our "Code Book," which explains that God has a "blueprint" for each of our lives. God made each one of us for a purpose, and through our Christian walk, we learn what

---

[46] Ibid.

God's plan is for our lives. Please do not confuse the term "codebook" to understand that the Bible has a secret code we are to decipher. The term codebook for our lives is similar to the Bible, being our manual for life. After speaking with my sister, I also remembered that the Bible has several examples of precise measurements for building certain items. Items, such as Noah's Ark (Genesis 6:14–16), the Ark of the Covenant (Exodus 25:10–22), God's Tabernacle in the desert (Exodus 26–27), the temple in Jerusalem (built by Solomon, 2 Chronicles 3–4), and the new Jerusalem (Revelation 21:10–27). In the book of Amos, we see the term plumb in two different ways. First as a construction term, such as

> Thus he shewed me: and, behold, the Lord stood upon a wall made by a plumbline, with a plumbline in his hand. (Amos 7:7 KJV)

And, as God's wrath against the people of Israel,

> And the Lord said to me, "What do you see, Amos?" And I said, "A plumb line." Then the Lord said, "Behold I am about to put a plumb line In the midst of My people Israel. I will not spare them any longer. (Amos 7:8 NASB)

The Bible describes the word level as a level path of righteousness or God leveling a path for His anger against the Egyptians while Moses tried to free the Hebrew people.

The way of the righteous is smooth; O Upright One, make the path of the righteous level. (Isaiah 26:7 NASB)

He leveled a path for His anger; He did not spare their souls from death, But turned their lives over to the plague. (Psalms 78:50 NASB)

The following passages explain a balanced God using the terms plumb and level, which tie it all together.

I will test you with the measuring line of justice and the plumb line of righteousness. Since your refuge is made of lies, a hailstorm will knock it down. Since it is made of deception, a flood will sweep it away. (Isaiah 28:17 NLT)

The God who made the world and everything in it, being Lord of heaven and earth, does not live in temples made by man, nor is he served by human hands, as though he needed anything, since he himself gives to all mankind life and breath and everything. (Acts 17:24–25 ESV)

Once again, we see God as positive and negative through the terms level and plumb. We seem to think God should view things humanly. We need to remember we are man, and He is God. God sees all things—past, present, and future—and knows all outcomes—we do not. God is level with the respect that He never changes, and His word never changes. We, however, are not level. We think we are, but our thinking process and emotions go all over the place—we are not level, not even close.

Throughout this chapter and this book, it will soon be revealed that our God does send unbelievers to the lake of fire for eternal punishment. However, please be reminded that you can be saved from the lake of fire before death; "Just as people are destined to die once, and after that to face judgment" (Hebrews 9:27 NIV), and if you only believe, "whosoever believeth" (John 3:16 KJV).

Let's explore what our Bible says about the Trinity.

A Triune God

"In the beginning" is a great place to start on the nature of God. A primary characteristic of God is that He is a plural (triune) God. In the original Hebrew translation of God, in this verse, is Elohim. Elohim is "the most frequent Hebrew word for

God, occurring over 2,200 times in the OT…Elohim is plural in sense as well as form…is the earliest name of God in the OT."[47]

The scriptures do not state "Triune God" or the word "Trinity," but it describes God as plural through Elohim.

Other passages describe God as plural.

And God said, Let us make man in our image,
after our likeness. (Genesis 1:26a KJV)

This verse is a beautiful representation of our triune God. He made us in His image and likeness. He did not make us gods; He made us as men (mankind—male and female). Since we are made in His image and likeness, why wouldn't we want to worship and obey Him? The words *"us"* and *"our"* prove a plural God.

The Old Testament continues showing us an Elohim God and is represented in this way.

And thou shalt love the Lord thy God with all thine
heart, and with all thy soul, and with all thy might.
(Deuteronomy 6:5 KJV)

Isaiah 9:6c "Eternal Father" (NASB).

The author James White gives us a basic definition of the Trinity.

---

[47] "Elohim" *Zondervan's Illustrated Bible Dictionary* Copyright © 1987, 2011 by Zondervan, retrieved from Biblegateway.com.

Within the One Being that is God, there exists eternally three coequal and coeternal persons, namely, the Father, the Son, and the Holy Spirit.[48]

Now we will jump to the New Testament scriptures that support a triune God. If you note, all these verses mention God, Jesus, and the Holy Spirit, representing each being in themselves and together.

> Go, therefore, and make disciples of all the nations, baptizing them in the name of the Father and the Son and the Holy Spirit. (Matthew 28:19 NASB)

> The grace of the Lord Jesus Christ, and the love of God, and the fellowship of the Holy Spirit, be with you all. (2 Corinthians 13:14 NASB)

> But ye, beloved, building up yourselves on your most holy faith, praying in the Holy Ghost, Keep yourselves in the love of God, looking for the mercy of our Lord Jesus Christ unto eternal life. (Jude 1:20–21 KJV)

> Additional scriptures support an Elohim God, such as:

> Thou shalt love the Lord thy God with all thy heart, and with all thy soul, and with all thy mind." (Matthew 22:37 KJV)

---

[48] James R. White, *The Forgotten Trinity* (Bloomington: Bethany House, 1998), 26.

✓ And, but not limited to, John 1:1, John 1:18, and 1 Corinthians 8:6.

Some passages show a singular God throughout the Bible, proving James White's definition of the Trinity. All three persons are distinct and together as one. This definition translates to mean that Jesus' deity is that He is God too. Therefore, those who choose to deny the trinity's existence diminish the deity of Jesus and the Holy Spirit's deity. To dive a little deeper into the theology of a Triune God is this: which Jesus do you believe in for your eternal salvation?

God is Sovereign

Simply put, God is sovereign means that God is in control. Yet, we might think there is nothing simple about it. Let's break this subject down into understandable terms. God is above all things and working through all things. He oversees all things in us and around us. God controls nature, including the warm sunlight, the cold of winter, and the stormy seas. Psalms 139 explains God's sovereignty (He is in control), omnipresence (He is always with us), and omniscience (He is all-knowing).

One might ask *Where is God in this pandemic, or why isn't He stopping rampant violence, sexual perversion, and murdering babies through abortion?* We need to trust that God is in control of all things; however, He deals with it differently than you or I. Because of God's all-knowing attribute, He knows the past, present, and future of all things—including all people. Further, God's divine wrath is not always immediate. His holy wrath might be on hold until judgment day. God's final wrath is for eternity—in the lake of fire.

The Lord has established His throne in the heavens, And His sovereignty rules over all. (Psalms 103:19 NASB)

The LORD hath prepared his throne in the heavens; and his kingdom ruleth over all. Bless the LORD, ye his angels, that excel in strength, that do his commandments, hearkening unto the voice of his word. Bless ye the LORD, all ye his hosts; ye ministers of his, that do his pleasure. Bless the LORD, all his works in all places of his dominion: bless the LORD, O my soul. (Psalms 103:19–22 KJV)

In an online article, Chip Ingram answered what the phrase "God is sovereign" meant. He discussed verses such as Revelation 21:6, Colossians 1:16, Romans 11:33, and Jeremiah 32:17. I found the following in his article especially helpful in describing God's sovereignty.

Romans 8:28 promises "that in all things God works for the good of those who love Him, who have been called according to His purpose" (NIV) … That's an amazing promise not only because it demonstrates that an all-powerful God cares about you and me, but because it cannot be fulfilled unless the One Who gives it is all-knowing, all-wise, all-powerful, and all-loving. The promise is a testimony to God's sovereignty.[49]

---

[49] Chip Ingram, "What does the phrase 'God is sovereign' really mean?" Christianity.com.

You will find the above article in full version on a link noted in the footnote below. While on the document, look for the sub-heading, *"How Does God's Sovereignty Impact My Everyday Life?"* Ingram's writings on God's Sovereignty assists us in understanding this attribute of God.

> In Ezekiel 18:3–4 (NIV), we read, "As surely as I live, declares the Sovereign Lord …" Job 38:4 (NASB) seems to sum it all up as well: "Where were you when I laid the foundation of the earth? Tell *Me*, if you have understanding."

> Our God is Lord over all!

Our awesome God has many attributes, as we are learning; however, for this book, I will focus on three key areas that describe Him to explain why a loving God would have a lake of fire with eternal torment. These three groups of His attributes also help us understand that He is a balanced God and further explains that He is sovereign.

Three Key Areas of God's Attributes

- His lovingkindness, grace, and mercy
- His justice and judgment
- His holiness and righteousness

A Biblical Retrospect of God's Attributes

His Lovingkindness, Grace, and Mercy

Numerous scriptures describe God in these areas of His attributes. While reading the verses below, I am sure you can relate and feel blessed.

> And God saw all that He had made, and behold, it was very good. And there was evening and there was morning, the sixth day. (Genesis 1:31 NASB)

The Bible also shares with us that God is good.

> You are good and do good; Teach me Your statutes. (Psalms 119:68 NASB)

I like how David said it.

> But You, Lord, are a compassionate and gracious God, Slow to anger and abundant in mercy and truth. (Psalms 86:15 NASB)

> Psalms 116:5a (NASB) reads, "Gracious is the Lord," and Psalms 103:8 (NASB) reads, "The LORD is compassionate and gracious, Slow to anger and abounding in mercy."

The scripture continues to describe God.

> The LORD is gracious and compassionate, slow to anger and rich in love. (Psalms 145:8 NIV)

> Or do you think lightly of the riches of His kindness
> and restraint and patience, not knowing that
> the kindness of God leads you to repentance?
> (Romans 2:4 NASB)

Throughout my life in churches and on Christian radio stations, I have heard that the difference between grace and mercy is that grace is receiving blessings we do not deserve while mercy is not receiving what we do deserve. However, before we can understand this, we must first realize that we are sinners needing redemption through Jesus Christ.

His Justice and Judgment

These areas of God's attributes seem to be puzzling or mysterious. How could a God full of lovingkindness pass eternal judgment on us? Simply put, He is who He is—the "I AM" (Exodus 3:14). God's wrath is divine and perfect.

I have learned throughout my life from sermons, listening to the Christian radio stations, and various devotionals that judgment can be both positive and negative. "The Greek word *mišpāṭ*, is "generally rendered 'justice' or 'judgment.'"[50] Further, "the term *mišpāṭ* is found most often in prophetic literature and is used in a striking way in Isa 40:55, where *mišpāṭ* is tied to God's sovereign execution of world affairs. God's justice is always perfect, even when his plan baffles human understanding."[51] In the Book of Psalms, David sought out God's mercy many times to protect him and pass judgment on those who were

---

[50] "Justice," *Mounce's Complete Expository Dictionary of Old and New Testament Words,* Copyright © 2006 by William D. Mounce. Found through BibleGateway.com.
[51] "Justice," *Mounce's Complete Expository Dictionary*

his enemies. David tells of his plight and victories, such as in Psalms 9:6 (NASB) "The enemy has come to an end," and in Psalms 27:2 (NASB) "When evil doers come upon me to devour my flesh, My adversaries and my enemies, they stumbled and fell." In Psalms 38:19 (NASB), David explains, "But my enemies are vigorous *and* strong, And those who wrongfully hate me are many."

In David's case, God's justice was positive for David by protecting him from his enemies, whereas negative for his enemies.

> Let us review His justice and judgment in the following verses.

> The Rock! His work is perfect, For all His ways are just; A God of faithfulness and without injustice, Righteous and just is He. (Deuteronomy 32:4 NASB)

> As for God, His way is blameless; The word of the Lord is refined; He is a shield to all who take refuge in Him. For who is God, but the Lord? And who is a rock, except our God, The God who encircles me with strength And makes my way blameless? (Psalms 18:30–32 NASB)

Another way of looking at justice and judgment is to view it as God's Perfect Wrath. There are consequences for being unsaved sinners, disobedient, and rejecting God.

Lord, God of vengeance, God of vengeance, shine forth! (Psalms 94:1 NASB)

O Lord, the God Who punishes, God Who punishes, let Your light shine! (Psalms 94:1 NLV)

A jealous and avenging God is the Lord, The Lord is avenging and wrathful. The Lord takes vengeance on His adversaries, And He reserves wrath for His enemies. (Nahum 1:2 NASB)

The wrath of God is being revealed from heaven against all the godlessness and wickedness of people, who suppress the truth by their wickedness. (Romans 1:18 NIV)

But because of your stubbornness and unrepentant heart you are storing up wrath for yourself on the day of wrath and revelation of the righteous judgment of God. (Romans 2:5 NASB)

But for those who are self-seeking and do not obey the truth, but obey unrighteousness, there will be wrath and fury. (Romans 2:8 ESV)

In flaming fire taking vengeance on them that know not God, and that obey not the gospel of our Lord Jesus Christ. (2 Thessalonians 1:8 KJV)

In order that they all may be judged who did not believe the truth, but took pleasure in wickedness. (2 Thessalonians 2:12 NASB)

The following scripture tells us of the judgment of Sodom and Gomorrah and the surrounding cities.

> Then the Lord rained brimstone and fire on Sodom and Gomorrah from the Lord out of heaven. (Genesis 19:24 NASB)

> Just as Sodom and Gomorrah and the surrounding cities, which likewise indulged in sexual immorality and pursued unnatural desire, serve as an example by undergoing a punishment of eternal fire. (Jude 1:7 ESV)

Let us move on to the third key point of God's attributes.

His Holiness and Righteousness

This third section serves two primary purposes. First, it describes that God is holy and righteous. Secondly, it ties the other two Key Areas of God's attributes together. God is not just a loving God, or just a God of judgment or only Holy, which helps us understand that He is a balanced God; you cannot have one without the other.

God Is Holy

> There is none holy as the LORD: for there is none beside thee: neither is there any rock like our God. (1 Samuel 2:2 KJV)

> Besides this, we have had earthly fathers who disciplined us and we respected them. Shall we

not much more be subject to the Father of spirits and live? For they disciplined us for a short time as it seemed best to them, but he disciplines us for our good, that we may share his holiness. (Hebrews 12:9–10 ESV)

Exalt the LORD our God, and worship at his holy hill; for the LORD our God is holy. (Psalms 99:9 KJV)

God Is Righteous

The Lord is righteous in all His ways, and holy in all his works. (Psalms 145:17 KJV)

Your testimonies are righteous forever; give me understanding that I may live. (Psalms 119;144 ESV)

The sum of your word is truth, and every one of your righteous rules endures forever. (Psalms 119:160 ESV)

Gracious is the Lord, and righteous; yea, our God is merciful. (Psalms 116:5 KJV)

The Almighty—we cannot find Him; He is exalted in power And He will not violate justice and abundant righteousness. (Job 37:23 NASB)

Because He is a holy and righteous God, He needs to be a God of justice and judgment (no sin can come before Him), or

His lovingkindness, grace, and mercy would be contradictory to His holiness and righteousness. All these attributes are under the umbrella of His sovereignty—He is in control. He is balanced.

God is in control, but we are not puppets or robots. God gave us free will. He wants us to love Him freely and willingly. Oh yes, God spiritually pulls on our heartstrings; He seeks us out first, but it is up to us to accept Him through His Son, Jesus.

Jesus made it clear.

> Jesus said to him, I am the way, and the truth, and the life; no one comes to the Father except through Me. (John 14:6 NASB)

> Here I am! I stand at the door and knock. If anyone hears my voice and opens the door, I will come in and eat with that person, and they with me. (Revelation 3:20 NIV)

> But nothing unclean will ever enter it, nor anyone who does what is detestable or false, but only those who are written in the Lamb's book of life. (Revelation 21:27 ESV)

Do All Roads Lead to the Same Place?

I have heard numerous people state that they could believe as they wanted to and that all paths led to the same place. People may believe in what they want; however, as for all roads leading to the same place—The Bible clearly says the opposite (Matthew 7:13–14; John 14:6).

I encourage those who believe in themselves or something other than the Bible—the Gospel of Jesus Christ—to consider the following.

- Are you sure you can save yourself for eternity? Perhaps you do not believe in eternity, which would equal hopelessness.
- What makes you feel you are so good that you do not need God?
- Are you sure what you believe is the truth? Have you measured up *your truth* with the Holy Bible's *truth*?

White explained this subject.

> There is no salvation in a false Christ. If we are to be united with Christ to have eternal life, then we must be united with the true Christ, not a false representation. It is out of love that Christ uttered John 8:24. We would do well to heed His words.[52]

> That is why I said that you will die in your sins; for unless you believe that I AM who I claim to be, you will die in your sins. (John 8:24 NLT)

We will now review an additional passage to answer the question: Do all paths lead to the same place?

> Enter through the narrow gate; for the gate is wide and the way is broad that leads to destruction, and there are many who enter through it. For

---

[52] White, *The Forgotten Trinity*, 104.

the gate is narrow and the way is constricted
that leads to life, and there are few who find it.
(Matthew 7:13–14 NASB)

Here is another powerful passage I would like all unbelievers to consider seriously.

For this reason also God highly exalted Him, and
bestowed on Him the name which is above every
name, so that at the name of Jesus EVERY KNEE
WILL BOW, of those who are in heaven and on
earth and under the earth, and *that* every tongue
will confess that Jesus Christ is Lord, to the glory
of God the Father. (Philippians 2:9–11 NASB)

According to scripture, all paths do not lead to the same place. The only way to heaven is through Jesus Christ (Matthew 7:13–14, John 3:16; John 14:6, Revelation 21:27). There is no eternal assurance in self-centered faiths. Ensure you are headed in the right direction and walking on the right path, i.e., the *narrow* path.

Unbelievers: What If You Are Wrong?

This section is also for believers in conditionalism and universalism. Additionally, this section covers other nontraditional, nonbiblical afterlife beliefs and religions.

What if all of you are wrong? You will have led generations to believe there are no eternal consequences for their sins.

On the contrary, there is eternal punishment in the eternal fire because that is what the Bible says.

Yes, even the thought of eternal consequences for one's soul in the lake of fire is horrific, and Jesus gave Himself sacrificially on the cross to save us from it.

Let us assume the traditionalists are right; at least, people are given hope and salvation. In other words, a person might think, *I choose Christ versus going to hell.* With just mere death, there is no hope. It leaves little or no room for an incentive to want to know Christ as a personal Savior. If one is just going to die, who cares? Most of the world thinks that anyway. Additionally, they do not want to be judged by God or anyone else for how they believe or live. They want to do their own will, not God's will, for their lives.

Most importantly, people should want to know Christ of their own free will because of His immense love for them, not because they want to avoid going to hell, though that is a good reason. Eternity with God will be much better than eternal punishment in the lake of fire. That is why it is vitally imperative and the believers' responsibility to share God's message with the unbelievers by obeying the Great Commission as referenced in Matthew 28:19–20.

The following two scenarios are not original, as I have heard them in sermons throughout my life, even from my father. Therefore, I present the following two scenarios in my own words.

Scenario One

Let us say there is only death at the end of our physical

lives. We will also assume there is no God the Father, God the Son, or God the Holy Spirit to believe. Let's also say there is no eternal life in heaven or eternal punishment in the lake of fire, thus just death.

Would Christians suffer for being Christians during their lives or in the afterlife in this scenario? No. Christians would have believed in the Bible, God, and redemption through Jesus Christ and then just die. Unbelievers would live their lives as they wanted to and then just die as well. No one suffers, and no one goes to an eternal destination—heaven or the lake of fire. Sounds good, doesn't it? No consequences, no suffering, nothing to lose for believers or unbelievers alike. But is that the truth?

Let us examine the flip side of this scenario.

Scenario Two

We will assume the traditional Christians are right—God exists, the Bible is the truth, and unsaved sinners (unbelievers) will be saved only through redemption in Jesus Christ. Let us accept there is a heaven and a lake of fire, eternal destinations for souls. If your name is in the Book of Life, you will be in heaven for eternity, but if your name is not in the Book of Life, you will be in the lake of fire for eternity.

Would Christians suffer for being Christians during their lives or in the afterlife in this scenario? No. Christians would be rewarded with eternal life in heaven. However, the unbelievers would be eternally tormented in the lake of fire.

In scenario two, unbelievers would have enormous eternal consequences. Is your unbelief worth it? Only you can answer that spiritual question. To answer that question, I suggest you turn to the Word of God. "A living hope" (v3) and sure salvation, the Bible offers this hope for believers in the following scripture (1 Peter 1:1–9 NASB). Specifically, we have "an inheritance *which is* imperishable, undefiled and will not fade away, reserved in heaven for you" (1 Peter 1:4 NASB).

Now we will examine further the two scenarios by including conditionalism and universalism in the equation. Advocates for these two views have led people to believe there are no eternal consequences for their unbelief; therefore, no incentive to receive salvation. Some may think *I'm just going to die or go through a purification process and eventually get to heaven anyway; why care about how I live now or whether I'm saved before my death?*

I am sincerely not trying to mock anyone's viewpoint or belief, but a person will be facing a grave dilemma. Just think about Judgment Day, and those who thought they were going to die or go through a purification process find out that no, they are going to the lake of fire for eternal punishment. The above is meant as a spiritual reality check of what will happen. This portrayal might seem insensitive, but our souls' eternal destinations are not a laughing matter.

In all sincerity and fairness, we know that all persons do decide to follow Christ or not. Therefore, it is not the fault of people who share their beliefs and viewpoints regarding the lake of fire. However, as Christians, we have a responsibility and need to be incredibly careful about what we share with unbelievers. We must share the gospel of Jesus Christ with the unbelieving world in a caring, loving, and truthful way, but we do not take responsibility for unbelievers' responses. Further, as Christians, we are accountable for sharing the Gospel and teaching and mentoring others, whether believers or unbelievers, with their spiritual growth and knowledge. In other words, we need to step up and *mend* our broken world. The following passage assists us in understanding this concept.

> For whosoever shall call upon the name of the Lord shall be saved. How then shall they call on him in whom they have not believed? and how shall they believe in him of whom they have not heard? and how shall they hear without a preacher? And how shall they preach, except they be sent? as it is written, How beautiful are the feet of them that preach the gospel of peace, and bring glad tidings of good things! (Romans 10:13–15 KJV)

In the book, *The Hole in our Gospel,* Stearns highlights his quote.

> In our evangelistic efforts to make the good news accessible and simple to understand, we seem to have boiled it down to a kind of "fire insurance" that one can buy...We've got our "ticket" to the next life.[53]

Stearns further emphasizes:

---

[53] Taken from page 5, *The Hole in Our Gospel 10th Anniversary Edition* by Richard Stearns Copyright © 2019 by Richard Stearns. Used by permission of Thomas Nelson. www.thomasnelson.com

There is a real problem with this limited view of the kingdom of God; it is not the whole gospel. Instead, it's a gospel with a gaping hole. First, focusing almost exclusively on the afterlife reduces the importance of what God expects of us in this life. The kingdom of God, which Christ said is "within you" (Luke 17:21 NKJV), was intended to change and challenge everything in our fallen world in the here and now. It was not meant to be a way to leave the world but rather the means to actually redeem it.[54]

I appreciate Stearns's precise portrayal of how we may present the gospel to the world, which sometimes lacks the full meaning. We need to concern ourselves with sharing the gospel to our broken world, not just making sure we are saved and leave it at that. We are to follow the great commission until we are no longer part of this world. I also feel that we need to be showing others how to spread the accurate "good news" of Jesus Christ. When we search the scriptures, we learn what the Bible tells us about Jesus. Jesus explains it to us.

> You search the Scriptures because you think that in them you have eternal life; and it is they that bear witness about me. (John 5:39 ESV)

We plant spiritual seeds in the unbelieving world; it is the Holy Spirit's role to convict hearts; we are the messengers. Therefore, we need to share the correct message of truth and hope in a caring and loving way.

---

[54] Ibid.

Chapter Summation

If the world is right, then there is nothing to worry about for the unbelievers. However, if the world is wrong, there is much to fear—eternal punishment for the unbelievers.

Additionally, it takes a leap of faith no matter what you believe. In other words, it takes a leap of faith to believe in Atheism because those who think there are no deities cannot concretely prove it. However, even though there are documented accounts in other books that match the Bible, it still takes a leap of faith to believe the Bible is the truth.

Therefore, I would instead take a leap of faith to accept God's promise of salvation through Jesus Christ and live eternally in heaven than to believe in something that promises nothing (i.e., we just die and go into the ground?). What do you choose to believe? Where is your leap of faith going to take you after death? Heaven or hell?

God is not just a god like those of Rome, Greece, or Egypt. God is not just a god; He is a just God, a God of justice and judgment. Unfortunately, these attributes of God are an area not very well liked or accepted by humanity. We seem only to receive his lovingkindness, grace, and mercy, but we do not want to believe in His justice or judgment. Some believe in God's divine judgment, yet they think that the judgment is the cessation of body and soul, not an eternal torment of any kind.

Through God's attributes, we learn about His nature and character, which describes Him as balanced. God loves us with open arms. The perfect example of this love is what Jesus did on the cross for us—His arms were open wide, and He took everyone's sin upon Himself. Oh, what grace and hope we have through Him.

He is God! He is the "I AM" God (Exodus 3:14).

> "A just God and a Savior, *There* is none beside Me." (Isaiah 45:21 NKJV)

Next up is exploring what the scriptures say about the lake of fire.

CHAPTER 3

The Lake of Fire

Defining the Lake of Fire through Scripture
Is it Real or just a Metaphor?

CHAPTER 3

The Lake of Fire

An Overview

I have had many discussions about my faith in Jesus Christ and the Holy Bible with others. At times, those I share my beliefs with believe in heaven but not hell, and they believe in Jesus but not in a triune God. Some consider hell to be just a metaphor, but they believe in heaven. I explain to such individuals that the apostle John described heaven and hell quite well in the Book of Revelation.

During my discussions, I shared that we cannot have a real heaven but have a metaphorical hell. If heaven is *real*, hell needs to be *real* too. If both are metaphors, Jesus died in vain. If there was no eternal torment, why would we need to be saved? And if neither heaven nor hell exists, the Bible would be a work of fiction, which most of the world believes anyway.

The most important conversation the young woman at work and I had was regarding hell. We had many discussions on the subject over four months.

The following is a summary of the young woman's beliefs. She explained that we create our hell of pain and suffering here on earth through the results of decisions and choices we've made. She further shared some individuals currently have their hell of mental illness and addiction, for example. Additionally, she stated that because God would not have eternal torment, evil souls just die. If one is saved through Jesus Christ, they will either go to heaven [if chosen to live in heaven] or live on an earthly paradise.

I have heard the following quote in several versions but did not know its origin. Yet with a bit of research, I found the author. You may have heard it as well. The quote comes from the book *Heaven* by Randy Alcorn.

> The best of life on earth is a glimpse of Heaven; the worst of life is a glimpse of Hell. For Christians, this present life is the closest they will come to Hell. For unbelievers, it is the closest they will come to Heaven.[55]

Alcorn said it best, and his quote helps us understand the Biblical theology that there is a heaven and a hell, and neither one is on earth. I concur with Alcorn, and I adopted and developed a spin-off quote that helps us understand this analogy: for believers, earth is the worst hell they will ever experience, whereas, for unbelievers, this earth is the best heaven they will ever experience.

Apostle John was describing the lake of fire in the Book of Revelation, not hell.

---

[55] Some content taken from page 28, *Heaven* by Randy Alcorn. Copyright © 2004. Used by permission of Tyndale House Publishers, a Division of Tyndale House Ministries. All rights reserved.

And death and hell were cast into the lake of fire.
This is the second death. (Revelation 20:14 KJV)

Along similar lines, the Bible discusses we need to be aware of false doctrine. For example, there are those who "have left the path of truth, claiming that the resurrection of the dead has already occurred; in this way, they have turned some people away from the faith" (2 Timothy 2:18 NLT). However, suppose we stay in the true faith. In that case, scriptures assure us, "Therefore, if anyone cleanses himself from these *things*, he will be an implement for honor, sanctified, useful to the Master, prepared for every good work" (2 Timothy 2:21 NASB).

Biblical Warning Signs

The Old and New Testaments give us multiple signs and prophesy about Jesus, the lake of fire, and its descriptions. A few brief examples are, we will have a savior coming: Isaiah 9:6 (NASB) tells us "for a child will be born to us," meaning "Immanuel" Isaiah 7:14 (NASB), and Isaiah 66:24 (NLT) says, "...For the worms that devour them will never die, and the fire that burns them will never go out." Throughout the New Testament, Jesus provides many warnings; one such example is Jesus explains in Matthew 25:31–46 (KJV), "everlasting fire" and "everlasting punishment." Do we listen?

The following analogy is not original; I have heard it in many forms throughout my life. Let us say you are taking a vacation with your family. As you drive, you start to see warning signs that the bridge is out—take an alternative route—cliff ahead. Would you go anyway and drive your family off the cliff, or would you heed the warnings and divert? Why is that different from biblical warnings about the lake of fire? We are not only given warning signs; we are also given an alternative route— Jesus Christ!

Defining the Lake of Fire through Scripture

Key Areas of This Chapter

- What is the lake of fire?
- How long will it last?
- Who will be in it?

Let us see what the Bible says about it.

What is the Lake of Fire?

- Revelation 19:20 (NASB) describes the lake of fire as "burns with brimstone."
- Revelation 19:20 (NIV) calls it "the fiery lake of burning sulfur."

The lake of fire is the second death.

- Revelation 21:8 (NASB): "The lake that burns with fire and brimstone, which is the second death."
- Revelation 20:14 (KJV): "And death and hell were cast into the lake of fire. This is the second death."

The lake of fire is described as the abyss or bottomless pit.

And the fifth angel blew his trumpet, and I saw a star fallen from heaven to earth, and he was given the key to the shaft of the bottomless pit. He opened the shaft of the bottomless pit, and from the shaft rose smoke like the smoke of a great furnace, and the sun and the air were darkened with the smoke from the shaft. (Revelation 9:1–2 ESV)

✓ Revelation 9:1–2 (NIV) reads "abyss" instead of the "bottomless pit."

How long will it last, and Who will be in it?

The scripture answers these questions; in fact, God's Word links the answers together. The scriptures state that the lake of fire is eternal torment.

What does the Bible mean when it says "eternal"? Are there different definitions of eternal that perhaps mean temporary? No. Eternal means eternal. The Hebrew word is "Ôlām, which refers to 'duration.'"[56] Below is an explanation for eternal.

Eternal—This word—and its synonyms "everlasting," "forever"—sometimes refer simply to a long time (e.g., Gen. 17:8; 2 Sam. 7:16). When applied to God, his words, and his acts, however, it clearly signifies the eternal and everlasting in the literal and absolute sense of the term. In the NT, its most common use is in the phrase "eternal life," which mingles future and present: it indicates

____

[56] "Eternal," *Zondervan Illustrated Bible Dictionary.* Retrieved from Biblegateway.com.

not only endless duration, but also divine quality
(Matt. 25:46; Jn. 3:16; 17:3).[57]

The Greek word for eternal is îlām, which means ancient, eternal, forever, everlasting.[58]

I will start with words right from the mouth of the perfect source—Jesus, who said it best in His Word. There is no question as to the time frame of either heaven or the lake of fire. Read Matthew 25:31–46 and specifically verse 46: "These will go away into eternal punishment, but the righteous into eternal life" (NASB). Jesus' words are clear.

Clarifying Revelation 14:9–11

Let's review additional scripture regarding eternal torment in the lake of fire. Throughout my life and during my online research regarding the three viewpoints, I came across various interpretations regarding Revelation 14:9–11. First, some believe that there would not be an eternal lake of fire because the holy angels and the Lamb would not be standing for an eternity viewing the burning smoke. Second, others understood the scripture to be metaphorical, and third, some just believe it means complete annihilation. Before we start, let's review what the scriptures say.

And the third angel followed them, saying with
a loud voice, if any man worship the beast and

---

[57] "Eternal," *Essential Bible Dictionary*. Copyright © 2011 by Zondervan. Retrieved from Biblegateway.com.

[58] "Eternal," Mounce, *Complete Expository Dictionary*, Retrieved from Biblegateway.com

his image, and receive his mark in his forehead, or in his hand, The same shall drink of the wine of the wrath of God, which is poured out without mixture into the cup of his indignation; and he shall be tormented with fire and brimstone in the presence of the holy angels, and in the presence of the Lamb: And the smoke of their torment ascendeth up forever and ever: and they have no rest day nor night, who worship the beast and his image, and whosoever receiveth the mark of his name. (Revelation 14:9–11 KJV)

This passage says in the "presence of the holy angels, and in the presence of the Lamb," but that does not mean those entities are standing there forever. Scripture says that those who took the mark "shall be tormented with fire and brimstone in the presence of the holy angels and in the presence of the Lamb." Then it tells us, "And the smoke of their torment ascendeth up for ever and ever …" but it does not state that the Lamb and the holy angels are standing there forever watching the smoke. The scriptures inform us that those who worship the beast and take his mark will be receiving God's wrath in the presence of the holy angels and the Lamb.

Yes, the smoke is eternal, the scriptures do not lie, and yes, the scriptures state in the presence of the Lamb and holy angels. However, it does not indicate that the Lamb and holy angels are standing there 24/7, watching the smoke of their torment. Indeed, their smoke is forever because their torment is eternal; however, the holy angels and the Lamb will not be standing there forever. According to scripture, they will initially see those entities thrown into the furnace and will watch their torment. Scriptures do not tell us that they will be watching the smoke of their torment forever; scriptures tell us the smoke of their torment is forever.

Another thought to consider, we do not know the configuration of heaven or the views the holy angels and the Lamb have of the eternal furnace. Still, if the Bible says the smoke of their torment rises forever, we must trust the Bible. One could reasonably think that if the smoke of their torment ascends forever and ever, then there is a possibility that the smoke of their torment could be seen by the holy angels and the Lamb eternally. Still, they will not be standing there forever watching the smoke.

In this case, I can see how one can interpret the scriptures to infer their meaning. Additionally, we need to be careful; we are not *reading into scripture what is not there.* The Word of God does not always tell us everything about everything; some things are a mystery. The important thing we must understand is what the Bible tells us is the truth.

I would like to discuss another aspect regarding the inference that the Lamb and holy angels are standing and watching. The Lamb, Jesus, can be in more than one place because of His attribute, omnipresence (Psalms139:7–10), as He is part of the Triune God. My take on "standing there" is this: even though God created man in His own image, He did not create man as gods. On the flip side, God is not a man; He is spiritual. God is not *just* a god; He is God. To infer that God is "standing there" leads me to believe some may be referring to God as a man who can be in only one place at one time. Not so. God is omnipresent.

As for the angels, they are beings created by God, and therefore, not omnipresent. However, God assigns angels various duties, which do include some earthly visits. An example, God sent angels to Sodom and Gomorrah to take Lot and his family away (Genesis 19:15) before God destroyed those regions (Genesis 19:24, Luke 17:29, Jude 7). Another occurrence, an Angel, came to protect Daniel when he was thrown into the lion's den (Daniel 6:6–22). Angels do have better things to do than just standing around watching tormenting smoke for eternity; however, there is a possibility that God could have assigned some of the holy angels to stand and watch forever. The referenced scripture above does not state "all the holy angels;" it says, "the holy angels." But we need to be careful because the Bible does not tell us this, yet it is possible. As I stated earlier, some things in the Bible are a mystery. A couple of examples are Daniel and Apostle John were both told to keep things secret or to seal certain things they saw in visions or what they heard. Daniel was told to "keep the vision secret" (Daniel 8:26 NASB), and John was told to "seal up the things which the seven peals of thunder have spoken, and do not write them" (Revelation 10:4 NASB).

Angels have various duties and responsibilities, such as but not limited to praising and serving God, delivering God's messages, and, as stated above, attend to specific tasks on earth. Not all angels are the same. God created different types, such as holy angels, cherubim, seraphim, cherubs, the angel(s) of the Lord, and there is Michael, an archangel. Each class of angels has a different look and duty. If anyone is interested in or has questions about angels, some excellent resources are

Angels Revised by Billy Graham, *Angels* by David Jeremiah, and the Book of Ezekiel.

Traditionalists usually view this passage to clarify that the lake of fire is indeed forever and that there is eternal torment, for the scriptures tell us that the smoke of their torment ascendeth up forever and ever.

The third angel mentioned in Revelation 14:9–11 "clears up some additional false assumptions—namely, that hell is not real, that hell is not forever, and that hell is merely a metaphor for the unpleasant things that happen to us on earth."[59]

Forever means forever; it does not mean anything but forever. So, if the Bible meant the smoke of their torment was temporary, then the Bible <u>would have</u> stated, *"their torment was temporary, then they were annihilated (or will go through a purification process), and then their smoke ascended up temporarily."*

Therefore, the scriptures inform us that the lake of fire is eternal torment, but the scriptures do not tell us that the Holy angels and the Lamb eternally stand there watching.

Continuing with—Who Will be in It, and How Long Will It Last?

> And the beast was taken, and with him the false
> prophet that wrought miracles before him, with
> which he deceived them that had received the
> mark of the beast, and them that worshipped
> his image. These both were cast alive into a

---

[59] Taken from page 154, *You Can Understand the Book of Revelation*, Copyright © 2011/2020 by Skip Heitzig. Published by Harvest House Publishers, Eugene, Oregon 97408, www.harvesthousepublishers.com

lake of fire burning with brimstone. (Revelation 19:20 KJV)

Then the devil, who had deceived them, was cast into the lake of fire and brimstone, where the beast and the false prophet are, and shall be tormented day and night for ever and ever. (Revelation 20:10 KJV)

And death and hell were cast into the lake of fire. This is the second death. (Revelation 20:14 KJV)

And whosoever was not found written in the book of life was cast into the lake of fire. (Revelation 20:15 KJV)

But fearful, and unbelieving, and the abominable, and murderers, and whoremongers, and sorcerers, and idolaters, and all liars, shall have their part in the lake which burneth with fire and brimstone: which is the second death. (Revelation 21:8 KJV)

I feel that the saddest passage about the lake of fire is the following.

In flaming fire, inflicting vengeance on those who do not know God and on those who do not obey the gospel of our Lord Jesus. They will suffer the punishment of eternal destruction, away from the presence of the Lord and from the glory of his might. (2 Thessalonians 1:8–9 ESV)

They are away from God, away from light, into the "outer darkness"—not terminated. Please read Matthew 8:12; 22:13; 25:30, which informs us of the "outer darkness." One cannot equate eternal torment with eternal life. Even Jesus said in Matthew 25:46 (NASB) "eternal punishment"; He did not say eternal life in the lake of fire. Heaven and hell are two different existences, but they are both infinite.

This world is sometimes cruel, dark, and ugly, but we still have the Lord our God with us. People can always turn to Him. Until their last breath, people can make a U-Turn toward God. However, those who have not chosen to follow Jesus before their last breath will end up in eternal torment and eternally away from God. Because their own choice to not follow Jesus keeps them in an eternally condemned sinful state—by their own free will—no more chances. This thought deeply saddens me, and I know it grieves our loving God.

However, scripture offers us hope.

> The one who believes in the Son has eternal life;
> but the one who does not obey the Son will not
> see life, but the wrath of God remains on him.
> (John 3:36 NASB)

> Then Jesus again spoke to them, saying, "I am
> the Light of the world; the one who follows Me will
> not walk in the darkness, but will have the Light
> of life." (John 8:12 NASB)

Is It Real or Just a Metaphor?

How does all this add up? Is the lake of fire real? Is it a metaphor? How can a loving God send people to the lake of fire?

Under Zondervan's definition of "death," I quote:

> The book of Revelation contains the expression "the second death" (Rev. 20:6, 14; 21:8); it is defined in symbolic terms as "the fiery lake of burning sulfur" (21:8) and is the opposite of "the crown of life" (2:10–11). It will be experienced by those whose names are not written in the Lamb's "book of life" (20:15) and means everlasting separation from God and his redeemed people.[60]

If I understand this interpretation correctly, I disagree. Zondervan's interpretation is that the lake of fire is eternal separation from God [only], for it appears he is excluding the eternal fire. Zondervan explains that the "fiery lake" is symbolic; others also believe that the lake of fire is symbolic (metaphorical). However, since the Bible does not contradict itself, I prefer to believe what Jesus said: "their fire will not be extinguished" (Mark 9:47–48 NASB), "the fire never goes out" (Mark 9:48 NLT), and "eternal fire" (Matthew 25:41 NASB). Jude 7 supports Jesus' words of eternal fire, and Isaiah 66:24 (NASB) tells us, "their fire will not be extinguished."

Jesus talked about hell as a real place, "the outer darkness." "In that place there will be weeping and gnashing of teeth"

---

[60] "Death," *Zondervan's Illustrated Bible Dictionary.* Retrieved from Biblegateway.com.

(Matthew 8:12 ESV). Jesus told us again about hell as the "unquenchable fire" (Mark 9:43 ESV). The lake of fire includes eternal separation from God, and it includes an eternal fire that is not quenched or extinguished. In the Old Testament, humanity was warned, "…their worm shall not die, their fire shall not be quenched…" (Isaiah 66:24 ESV).

God loves us, and His desire is not for us to spend eternity in the lake of fire. In Chapter 2, we learned that His attributes would not contradict each other. Scripture assures us He does not do this willingly.

> For He does not afflict willingly Or grieve the sons of mankind. (Lamentations 3:33 NASB)

> For he does not willingly bring affliction or grief to anyone. (Lamentations 3:33 NIV)

He takes no pleasure.

> Say to them, As surely as I live, declares the Sovereign Lord, I take no pleasure in the death of the wicked, but rather that they turn from their ways and live. Turn! Turn from your evil ways! Why will you die, people of Israel? (Ezekiel 33:11 NIV)

> Do I take any pleasure in the death of the wicked? Declares the Sovereign Lord. Rather, am I not pleased when they turn from their ways and live? (Ezekiel 18:23 NIV)

When the scriptures speak of "death," it is a spiritual death. For example, Adam and Eve disobeyed by eating the forbidden fruit, yet they did not die on the spot—they died a spiritual death and later a physical death because their souls are eternal.

The Rich Man and Lazarus

In Luke 16:19–31, Jesus was speaking. I will quote specific verses that describe Hades as a real place. Remember, "Death and Hades were thrown into the lake of fire" (Revelation 20:14 ESV). Those "whose name not found written in the book of life" (Revelation 20:15 NIV) will end up in eternal judgment; they will feel the pain: "their fire will not be extinguished (Mark 9:48 NASB).

The rich man died and was in Hades.

> In Hades he raised his eyes, being in torment, and saw Abraham far away and Lazarus in his arms. And he cried out and said, 'Father Abraham, have mercy on me, and send Lazarus so that he may dip the tip of his finger in water and cool off my tongue, for I am in agony in this flame. (Luke 16:23–24 NASB)

Additional Description of the Fire

The rich man was "in agony in this flame," yet if you read, he was communicating with Abraham, and the flame was not consuming him.

The book of Exodus informs us about a similar fire—a burning bush in front of Moses.

Then the angel of the Lord appeared to him in a blazing fire from the midst of a bush; and he looked, and behold, the bush was burning with fire, yet the bush was not consumed. (Exodus 3:2 NASB)

When the Lord saw that he turned aside to look, God called to him from the midst of the bush and said, "Moses, Moses!" And he said, "Here I am." (Exodus 3:4 NASB)

A similar yet different aspect of the fire: The pillar of fire was amid them; it was not consuming them.

And the Lord was going before them in a pillar of cloud by day to lead them on the way, and in a pillar of fire by night to give them light, so that they might travel by day and by night. (Exodus 13:21 NASB)
✓ Other scripture: Exodus 13:22; Numbers 14:14; Nehemiah 9:11, 9:19

Also, in Mark, Jesus described the fire that is not quenched/extinguished.

Their worm does not die, and their fire will not be extinguished. (Mark 9:48 NASB)

Of course, we cannot forget about Sodom and Gomorrah. The people did die a physical death, yet their souls are eternal.

And don't forget Sodom and Gomorrah and
their neighboring towns, which were filled with
immorality and every kind of sexual perversion.
Those cities were destroyed by fire and serve as
a warning of the eternal fire of God's judgment.
(Jude 7 NLT)

The fire emitted by the burning bush and the pillar of fire produced light. If anyone has ever built a campfire or a fire on the beach, they know of the light and feel the heat that it generates. This type of fire burns and destroys and eventually goes out as the wood burns up. The fire in the lake of fire is a different story. Scripture describes the lake of fire as outer darkness; therefore, the fire in the lake of fire does not transmit light, yet it is eternally burning and tormenting. This fire does not extinguish, and it causes eternal pain for the unbeliever. The lake of fire is far worse, I believe, than we can ever imagine as humans. Additionally, the lake of fire never runs out of fuel— the fuel being the unbeliever's bodies—"Their worm does not die, and their fire will not be extinguished" (Mark 9:48 NASB).

Some may think the above is shocking and sickening and try to dismiss it from their minds. Further, some would leave this part out of the gospel message when witnessing to others. The main reason for this is fear of the unknown. In introductory psychology, I learned the lack of knowledge produces fear. In other words, people are afraid of what they do not understand or things that are out of the norm. So, in this case, the more knowledge you acquire of God's Word will lessen your fear. Oh, we are to be in fear of hell, don't get me wrong. But we should not be afraid of sharing the whole gospel of Jesus Christ. We cannot "honey coat" the eternal judgment of hell. However, when we know that hell is God's divine wrath and there is an alternative place—heaven—to dwell for eternity, we can confidently share this message with others and not be petrified in doing so. Further, spiritually speaking, more important than knowledge of God's Word is trusting in God's Word—God's Word tells us only the truth.

The key to understanding this concept is the following: Jesus came to earth to die for our sins and save us from a horrifying eternity. The choice is ours to make, yet some continually choose to deny Christ even after knowing the truth.

In their book, *Short Answers to BIG Questions,* the Arnolds accurately describe hell.

> Yes, hell is indeed a real place. It is mentioned so many times throughout the Bible that we cannot ignore it, even if we want to. There are three things we can determine about hell from scripture: that it is a literal place, that it involves conscious torment, and that it is eternal.[61]

> Throughout scripture, hell is mentioned as a destination, a literal place for those who have sinned against God will go.[62]

> ✓ Additional passages: Revelation 20:10; Jude 7; Matthew 25:46; Mark 9:48.

Jesus informed us.

---

[61] Arnold, *Short Answers to BIG Questions*, 135–136.
[62] Ibid., 136.

And will come out: those who did the good *deeds* to a resurrection of life, those who committed the bad *deeds* to a resurrection of judgment." (John 5:29 NASB).

For comparison, I listed the same verse in a different translation.

And they will rise again. Those who have done good will rise to experience eternal life, and those who have continued in evil will rise to experience judgment. (John 5:29 NLT)

If you read John 5:28–30, you will better understand what Jesus is saying.

Chapter Summation

Through scripture, I have described what the Bible says about the lake of fire, how long it will last, and who will be in it.

The lake of fire is real; it is eternal with conscious torment. It is a horrific destination with no out after death, and God designed it.

Judgment day is coming, and no one is exempt from it. Some may feel immune and will not experience it if they do not believe in it. I am afraid for them, for they are in for a rude awakening as they will eventually be standing before God.

Fudge, a strong advocate for conditionalism and coauthor of *Two Views of Hell*, wrote, "God's judgment will be measured by perfect, holy, divine justice. Even hell will demonstrate the absolute righteousness of God."[63] Fudge is correct on God's divine justice; however, he believes that the lake of fire is complete annihilation, not eternal punishment.

For those who believe they need to be chosen to live in heaven for eternity, I have this to say to encourage you. When you become a believer, you are a child of God (John 1:12) and, therefore, chosen (NASB: 1 Peter 2:9 & Revelation 17:14). Your destination upon death (or the rapture) is an eternity in heaven with your Savior. Consequently, I question the reasoning of those who claim to love Jesus would rather live apart from Him. However, the Book of Revelation explains about a new heaven and new earth (Revelation 21:1, KJV) in our future. Since we will be changed in the twinkling of an eye (1 Corinthians 15:52, KJV), we will have the ability to go from heaven to earth. But our "mansions" will be in heaven. Praise the Lord!

The following scripture will help us understand that Jesus wants us in heaven with Him because He is preparing a place for us.

> In My Father's house are many rooms; if *that* were not *so*, I would have told you, because I am going *there* to prepare a place for you. And if I go and prepare a place for you, I am coming again and will take you to Myself, so that where I am, *there* you also will be. (John 14:2–3 NASB)

✓ The KJV says "many mansions."

Let us now continue our route to Chapter 4: "The Beauty of John 3:16."

---

[63] Fudge, *Two Views of Hell*, 21.

CHAPTER 4

The Beauty of John 3:16

Spiritually Defining John 3:16

"For God so Loved the World"

(John 3:16a KJV)

CHAPTER 4

The Beauty of John 3:16

An Overview

The following much-loved and referenced verse shares with us the beauty of God's love, grace, mercy, and lovingkindness toward us.

> For God so loved the world, that He gave His only begotten Son, that whosoever believeth in him should not perish, but have everlasting life. (John 3:16 KJV)

As a child, I learned John 3:16 in the King James Version. While writing this book, the Holy Spirit revealed to me a deeper understanding of this verse. I have had conversations and online dialogues with various people who shared that it was impossible to have a personal relationship with God. Some have said that Jesus had been an important part of their lives for many years; they were heartfelt and portrayed their strong faith in Jesus and genuinely believed the only way to eternal life was through Him.

That sounds like a personal relationship. Yet, I do question their statements. How could people consider that Jesus Christ is an essential part of their lives and not have a personal relationship with Him? God created us in His own image (Genesis 1:26) and walked with Adam and Eve daily in the Garden of Eden (Genesis 3:8 KJV). Thus, God initiated a personal relationship with humankind from the beginning and has carried it through to His Son, Jesus Christ.

Because of sin, we are separated from God, but through redemption in Jesus Christ, God's Son, we are cleansed from all unrighteousness (1 John 1:9 KJV). Jesus was clearly saying that He was the only way to the Father (John 14:6).

The Bible is all about God's relationship with humanity. Ever since that relationship was broken in the Garden of Eden, God has been trying to restore that relationship. He sent His Son to die on the cross to save us and mend that relationship.

Spiritual Daddy

God wants to have spiritual intimacy with us; He wants us to share our whole lives with Him and approach Him as His children (Luke 18:15–17). He is our Abba Father, our spiritual daddy. That is why He created us in His image (Genesis 1:26), and God has a perfect will for each of us.

> And do not be conformed to this world, but be transformed by the renewing of your mind, so that you may prove what the will of God is, that which is good and acceptable and perfect. (Romans 12:2 NASB)

Because you are sons, God has sent the Spirit
of His Son into our hearts, crying out, "Abba!
Father!" (Galatians 4:6 NASB)

Spiritually Defining John 3:16

For God so loved the world …

Love is part of a relationship, whether romantic love, parent-child love, or friendship love. God created us to worship Him. Worshiping God is part of the relationship, including prayer and reading His Word. God wants a personal spiritual intimacy with each of us. He wants us to share our lives with Him.

God does not want just a Sunday-morning relationship with us; He wants us to give Him our entire lives willingly and openly.

God so loved the world …that is the start of the best personal relationship with God one can ever hope to have.

… that He gave His only begotten Son …

God gave the world a gift, and in most relationships, gifts are given—wedding gifts, graduation gifts, birthday gifts, and anniversary gifts, for instance. Giving gifts to each other is a part of a relationship and shows that we care—it is a way of expressing our love to one another.

God gave us His most precious gift, His only begotten Son, to die on the cross a most horrific death (John 19:1–20). He became the sin of the world and shed His precious blood on Calvary's tree so that we might be saved.

- Hebrews 2:9 (NASB): "… by the grace of God He might taste death for everyone."
- Hebrews 12:2 (NASB): "… endured the cross, despising the shame."
- Philippians 2:8 (NASB): "He humbled Himself by becoming obedient to the point of death: death on a cross."

Jesus sacrificed Himself on the cross for our sake. His death was God's way of showing us He loved us. God's gift to us was Jesus Christ being the atonement for our sins, the perfect sacrifice. God opened His arms to the world in a loving gesture for us to come to Him just as He did through His Son, Jesus Christ, on the cross.

People may ask, Saved from what? What sin? To answer that question, let us turn to the scriptures.

> But God commendeth his love toward us, in that, while we were yet sinners, Christ died for us. (Romans 5:8 KJV)

> The next day John seeth Jesus coming unto him, and saith, Behold the Lamb of God, which taketh away the sin of the world. (John 1:29 KJV)

> … and he is the propitiation for our sins: and not for ours only, but also for the sins of the whole world. (1 John 2:2 KJV)

> All have sinned and come short of the glory of God. (Romans 3:23 ESV)

> For the wages of sin is death, but the gracious
> gift of God is eternal life in Christ Jesus our Lord.
> (Romans 6:23 NASB)

✓ ESV and NLT translations say "free gift" instead of "gracious gift."

… that whosoever believeth in Him should not perish …

Whosoever means you! When I was a child, I attended Sunday school and vacation Bible school. The teachers would tell us to personalize the verse, for example, "For God so loved Elisabeth." It is your turn to personalize the verse for you.

This part of the verse tells us to believe in Him so we will not perish. People ask, "How could a loving God send people to hell?" Well, we send ourselves to hell by not believing in Jesus Christ. Spiritually speaking, God does send the unbelievers to the lake of fire.

> And death and hell were cast into the lake of fire.
> This is the second death. And whosoever was
> not found written in the book of life was cast into
> the lake of fire. (Revelation 20:14–15 KJV)

As I discussed in Chapter 1, some believe that the lake of fire is complete annihilation, and they also think that the word *perish* means just death and death alone. However, the Bible tells us differently.

> In flaming fire, dealing out retribution to those
> who do not know God, and to those who do not
> obey the gospel of our Lord Jesus. These people

will pay the penalty of eternal destruction, away from the presence of the Lord and from the glory of His power. (2 Thessalonians 1:8–9 NASB)

Now comes the essential part of this beautiful verse of God's love for us. He does not want us to perish in the lake of fire forever. He wants us to be in heaven with Him; however, we need to believe in His Son, Jesus Christ. Scriptures assure us,

> That if you confess with your mouth Jesus *as* Lord, and believe in your heart that God raised Him from the dead, you will be saved. (Romans 10:9 NASB)

> Whoever confesses that Jesus is the Son of God, God remains in him, and he in God. (1 John 4:15 NASB)

> If anyone acknowledges that Jesus is the Son of God, God lives in them and they in God. (1 John 4:15 NIV)

> ✓ ESV says, "abides in," and KJV says, "dwells in," instead of "remains in" or "lives in" (NASB and NIV, respectfully).

The essential elements of this section are believing and choosing to accept or reject Jesus. If we believe, we will have eternal life; however, as John 3:18 (KJV) informs us, "he that believeth not is condemned already," and therefore, already judged.

… but have everlasting life.

The best part of God's personal relationship with believers is eternity with Him. To back up this part with other scriptures,

> He that hath the Son hath life; and he that hath not the Son of God hath not life. (1 John 5:12 KJV)

> These things I have written to you who believe in the name of the Son of God, so that you may know that you have eternal life. (1 John 5:13 NASB)

> so that, as sin reigned in death, so also grace would reign through righteousness to eternal life through Jesus Christ our Lord. (Romans 5:21 NASB)

> I love what Jesus himself told us.

> Truly, truly, I say to you, the one who believes has eternal life. (John 6:47 NASB)

Some Areas of Concern Regarding Salvation of "Special" Situations

I know some are concerned and question salvation or the opportunity of salvation for unusual circumstances. Therefore, I have divided them into three main groups.

- Innocent babies and children
- Those who perhaps have not heard the gospel
- Those who died before Christ came to die for our sins

In this chapter, I will address the first area of concern, Innocent Babies and Children. The other two categories will be discussed in Chapter 5, "Jesus' Descent to Hades."

I will share my understanding to show that God has all these areas considered in His Word because He loves us dearly.

Innocent Babies and Children

One might ask, "What about the innocent babies and children?" However, I believe God has all this taken care of because He is a gracious and amazing God.

This subject is sensitive, and there are many varying beliefs. Therefore, we must take the time to discuss this subject.

An example, the scripture does not explicitly state that infants and children are automatically saved. After Adam and Eve sinned in the Garden of Eden, all were born into condemnation, but scripture tells us how God feels about and takes care of infants and children.

We must look to the scriptures to find our answer. The first passage that came to my mind regarding children and babies was this.

> People were also bringing babies to Jesus for him to place his hands on them. When the disciples saw this, they rebuked them. But Jesus called the children to him and said, *Let the little children come to me and do not hinder them, for*

the kingdom of God belongs to such as these. Truly I tell you, anyone who will not receive the kingdom of God like a little child will never enter it. (Luke 18:15–17 NIV)

✓ Additional scripture: Matthew 18:1–14, 19:14–15; Mark 10:13–16

I love the story about Hagar. God looked out for her by sending an angel to her in the desert. Here is the story in a nutshell.

Sarai had given her handmaiden, Hagar, to her husband Abram to have a baby through Hagar. Hagar conceives, yet trouble happens. Hagar brags about being able to conceive and not Sarai, which belittles Sarai. In other words, Hagar was disrespectful to Sarai. Sarai gets jealous and treats Hagar harshly. So, Hagar runs away to the desert toward Shur [near Egypt]. An angel speaks to her and asks her questions about where she is going. The angel tells her to go back to Sarai and submit to her. Now, some of you might think, why on earth would she go back and be poorly treated. Hagar needed to submit to Sarai's authority respectfully. Further, in all reality, God was protecting her and her unborn son, Ishmael. "The angel of the Lord also said to her, 'I will greatly multiply your descendants so that they will be too many to count.'" (Genesis 16:10 NASB)

You can find the story in Genesis 16:1–12. I suggest checking out the following translations: NASB, ESV, NIV, NLT, NKJV, and KJV—it is an interesting story.

I also looked at other books written about the subject, including *40 Questions about Heaven and Hell*. Author Alan Gomes brought to our attention other scripture that shows us "that God has a relationship with infants,"[64] including Psalms 22:9–10, 13:13, 71:6, Jeremiah 1:4–5, and Luke 1:15–16.

Gomes ties it all together in a sensitive manner.

God saves infants on the same basis as adults, and that is through Christ dying for their sins on the cross and rising from the dead in order to impart new life to them.[65]

Gomes further shared, "As Augustine once well stated,"[66] Jesus is Jesus even to infants, granting that his name means "Jehovah saves."[67]

Christ's death is the sole provision by which satisfaction to the divine wrath may be made for sin, whether for an infant or for an adult.[68]

Gomes concluded with, "…even if we do not have as much information on this topic as we might wish, we can be satisfied

---

[64] Alan W. Gomes, *40 Questions about Heaven and Hell* (Grand Rapids: Kregel Academics, 2018), 102.

[65] Gomes, *40 Questions*, 106.

[66] Ibid.

[67] Augustine, *On Marriage and Concupiscence* 2.60, quoted in Alan W. Gomes, *40 Questions about Heaven and Hell* (Grand Rapids: Kregel Academics, 2018), 106.

[68] Gomes, *40 Questions*, 106.

that we have a just and merciful God in whom we can place our absolute trust."[69] I think Gomes wrapped this section up beautifully. We must fully trust that God will take care of the innocent, and they will be in His arms for eternity.

An Upcoming Article: Biblically Justifying The Sanctity of Life

An Overview

Before I begin, I would like to offer a friendly reminder that I am not judging anyone or trying to offend anyone. One of my goals is to provide solutions and channels of assistance. I will be describing what the Bible says about the shedding of Innocent Blood. We need to protect our children—unborn to full-term—for it seems they have no voice. Our innocent babies are the "voiceless" (Proverbs 31:8 NKJV, NLT). We, as the human race, need to protect them and therefore be their voice. I would also like to interject a couple of questions some may have: "Where is God in all this?" And "Why isn't He intervening?" God is indeed sovereign, but He does not control us like puppets or robots. God has given humanity "free will." Since the original sin in the Garden of Eden, humankind has given over to continued evil.

---

[69] Gomes, *40 Questions,* 107.

An Imminent Worldwide Curse:
Shedding of Innocent Blood

Our society and other countries worldwide are actively involved in an extensive heinous un-Godly action—infanticide = abortion. The statistics are more than overwhelming. Since 1980, the total abortions performed worldwide are more than, and escalating to an alarming total of 1,599,464,101 (mid-day 12/26/20) and increasing by the second.[70]

I will explain infanticide, "the crime of killing a child within a year of birth; the practice in some societies of killing unwanted children soon after birth; a person who kills an infant, especially their own child."[71] Infanticide is on the same level as abortion—Abortion is nothing less than the genocide of our unborn children.

The tragedy and the ultimate victims of abortion are two-fold: killing the innocent unborn child and the women who allow it to be done to their bodies. I sincerely feel that most women, especially young gals, do not precisely comprehend what they have done. I have heard misinformation through the years that the unborn child does not feel any pain from the abortion or that the fetus would not live outside of the womb, so it will not make a difference. This delusional perception is a horrific misleading justification for abortion for many. I believe there is some research out there that proves the unborn to full-term children do feel the pain. The idea the embryo or fetus cannot live outside of the womb is a poor misleading excuse and should have nothing to do with it because the embryo/fetus is

---

[70] www.numberofabortions.com

[71] "infanticide," Microsoft.bing

still a living human developing in a womb. This mindset shows a complete disregard for the sanctity of life. Scripture shows us a different perception of life in the womb, "You made all the delicate, inner parts of my body and knit me together in my mother's womb" (Psalms 139:13 NLT).

The ramifications of shedding innocent blood will haunt those women for the rest of their lives. The crime is: It appears our society and our judicial system have given no rights to the unborn child—no protection whatsoever—not just in the United States, but worldwide as well!

Examples are as follows.

> Russia legalized abortion in 1920. China legalized abortion to include other than medical issues in the early 1950s. Before 1971, India allowed abortions only due to the woman's health; currently, only up to 24 weeks without court approval.[72]

Humanity, as a whole, has adopted a cavalier and calloused attitude regarding the sanctity of life. Jesus foretold us this when He said, "Sin will be rampant everywhere, and the love of many will grow cold" (Matthew 24:12 NLT).

However, I passionately believe that there is a third segment of the crime and is a tragedy—the fathers of those unborn babies. Specifically, the fathers wanting to keep the babies, yet the mother chose death for the unborn child. It is overwhelmingly heartbreaking for many men who wanted their children to be born.

Let us take a look at God's feelings toward those who

---

[72] Abortions (specific countries) Wikipedia

murder children—shed innocent blood. We will go back in biblical time to an era of Jewish Kings, specifically, *the life of King Manasseh.*

> It indeed came upon Judah at the command of the LORD, to remove *them* from His sight due to the sins of Manasseh, in accordance with everything that he had done, and also for the innocent blood which he shed, for he filled Jerusalem with innocent blood; and the LORD was unwilling to forgive. (2 Kings 24:3–4 NASB)

I would like to give you a little background of the above passage, for I do not want just to drop off a verse and then walk away from it without an explanation. The story of Manasseh can be found in 2 Kings 21:1–18. Further back in the Old Testament, God gave us specific instructions regarding what not to do with our children.

> Do not permit any of your children to be offered as a sacrifice to Molech, for you must not bring shame on the name of your God. I am the LORD. (Leviticus 18:21 NLT)

One of the pagan gods was Molech. One description I heard in a sermon long ago: Molech was a bronze statue approximately five feet tall and had a hollowed-out belly. In the statue's belly, they would put wood and other items to create a fire, and the figure would become red hot. The statue had two arms with hands stretched out; the people would place the babies on those arms and hands. Some drummers would beat on drums to create great noise to drown out the crying of the babies. The practice of drowning out the crying was produced on purpose because people may regret what they have done if they heard the screaming babies. This pagan practice of child sacrificing was introduced by pagan worshipers, such as the Amalekites, Ammonites, and the Moabites.

The Lord gave King Saul instructions through the Prophet Samuel to completely wipe out the Amalekites, yet Saul did not obey (1 Samuel 15:1–23). Likewise, the Israelites did not start child sacrifices until King Solomon introduced the act (1 Kings 11:7). The following scripture references describe what King Manasseh did that was evil in the sight of the Lord.

> Manasseh also sacrificed his own sons in the fire in the valley of Ben-Hinnom. He practiced sorcery, divination, and witchcraft, and he consulted with mediums and psychics. He did much that was evil in the LORD's sight, arousing his anger. (2 Chronicles 33:6 NLT)

> Furthermore, Manasseh shed very much innocent blood until he had filled Jerusalem from one end to another, besides his sin into which he misled Judah, in doing evil in the sight of the LORD. (2 Kings 21:16 NASB)

"So the Lord spoke to Manasseh and his people, but they paid no attention" (2 Chronicles 33:10 NASB). As a result of refusing to follow God's ways, God allowed them to be captured, and Manasseh was chained and taken off to Babylon (2 Chronicles 33:11 NASB). While Manasseh was in captivity, he went before the Lord and asked His forgiveness, and when he prayed to the Lord, the Lord was moved; God allowed him to be brought back to Jerusalem, and Manasseh knew the Lord *alone* is God (2 Chronicles 33:12–13 NASB). If you will read the following scripture reference in 2 Chronicles 33:14–20 (NASB), you will learn that Manasseh destroyed all the alters in the high places, gave "thanksgiving offerings," and "ordered Judah to serve the Lord God of Israel." This passage also tells of his prayer to God and discusses the end of his life. As an additional note, Manasseh was not the only King that was evil in the sight of the Lord. If you want to take the time to read 1 & 2 Chronicles and 1 & 2 Kings, you will have your eyes opened.

The above story of Manasseh's life is compelling because it shows us God's love for innocent babies and children. God stepped in by having Manasseh captured, which ultimately led him to confess and ask forgiveness. Manasseh stopped his evil ways and tore down the altars and idols. In other words, you do not mess with God's babies! The pagan ritual of child sacrificing is no different than killing babies through abortion. As you read the scripture offered, you will learn of the types of idols worshiped.

Along with idol worship comes sexual promiscuity through cult/temple prostitutes and the general population, thus unwanted babies. The idol Molech was used to kill those unwanted babies. Currently, sexual promiscuity is rapidly increasing in our world, and hence a continuation of unwanted babies. In today's society, we use abortion to kill unwanted babies. Since the United States Supreme Court decision of Roe v. Wade in 1973, over 62,479,438 (and increasing by the second, as of 12/26/20 mid-day) recorded babies killed through abortion.[73] For clarification, an exceedingly small percentage of abortions performed are due to the mother's health or from someone who had been raped. Even then, let God decide on decisions of life and death. I understand that this may be easier said than done. Yet, God knows all and sees all, even in the future. Some Pro-life doctors can assist and pray with you as you decide, especially when it is a medical issue with the baby or the mother. In any case, pray for God's guidance and search the scriptures to find your answer.

I am not insensitive to anyone's situation. There are millions of families that want to adopt babies and give them continued life. Some I understand are willing to pay for prenatal care and pay for room and board, even in some cases. It is also my understanding that the Fire Departments take babies without questions and some hospitals too. In addition, there are pro-life pregnancy care clinics and adoption agencies that can answer your questions and assist you in your decision to give your child continued life. A simple phone call to those entities can answer your questions.

Human life begins at conception, whether that life form can live outside the womb or not. It is not a cat or dog, nor is it an apple or an orange; what is growing in your womb is a human life. I find it difficult to understand the mindset that when a person does not want the baby, they consider it a clump of cells. If the pregnancy is wanted, they feel that growing in their womb is a baby and almost immediately decorates a nursery in preparation. I have never viewed the life form in the womb as a clump of cells. In the beginning stages after conception, the life form does look like a clump of cells, but it is still a life

---

[73] www.numberofabortions.com

form—human life form. If it is only a clump of cells, then why is there a heartbeat? A heartbeat can be heard as early as four to six weeks. Between ten and twelve weeks, the fetus looks like a miniature human being; during this time frame, most pro-life clinics or doctors can show you the *little baby* on an ultrasound machine—it is wonderfully unique!

Additionally, no one on God's green earth will ever convince me that those unborn to full-term babies that are aborted do not feel any pain. Even if we do not hear their pain, I know the Lord God above hears all their cries and painful groanings, and He sees every one of their tears! Was there a funeral? What was their name? Is there a gravesite to visit? Will they ever be remembered? One of the Ten Commandments was extremely clear.

> Thou shall not kill. (Exodus 20:13 KJV)
> You shall not murder. (Exodus 20:13 ESV, NASB, NIV, NKJV)
> You must not murder. (Exodus 20:13 NLT)

I have not found any exceptions in the Bible stating you can kill or murder your unborn to full-term baby if it is inconvenient or otherwise. Unfortunately, some judges in the court system aim to please man instead of pleasing God. Abortion is not women's health care; it is the modern version of child sacrificing. If the laws of our country are contrary to God's Word, then those laws are wrong. God does not sanction abortion—Satan does!

Abortions were not performed in biblical times and many years after, for they did not have the medical technology as we do now; therefore, the only means the people had to rid the society of unwanted babies was child sacrificing. However,

I would not be shocked if they did try different methods to remove the unwanted babies from their bodies because of how human nature is. Yet, it probably ended the life of the mother or created other health disasters. Therefore, no matter how child sacrificing is performed, it is still detestable and evil before God.

Before anyone starts yelling and screaming at me, *What do I know? As* I stated in my Introduction, I have had a journey of my own. I went through a crisis pregnancy during 1979-1980, and I have this to say: I chose life, and my *clump of cells* is now forty-one years old, and we are both doing fine. I told you it was a human life form in your womb! Deciding to keep my baby was one of the best decisions I have ever made, as the Lord *truly* bless me with my wonderful daughter, and I cannot imagine my life without her—I love her dearly. I never considered abortion! The other best decision was wanting to follow Jesus Christ! No, I am not perfect, and I am blessed to know and experience God's forgiveness (1 John 1:9). God does forgive, and He blesses us at the same time.

- "Go. From now on do not sin any longer." (John 8:11 NASB)
- "...there will be *more* joy in heaven over one sinner who repents than over ninety-nine righteous people who have no need of repentance." (Luke 15:7 NASB)
- "...do not sin anymore, so that nothing worse happens to you." (John 5:14 NASB)
- And this same God who takes care of me will supply all your needs from his glorious riches, which have been given to us in Christ Jesus. (Philippians 4:19 NLT)

We always had a roof over our heads, food on the table, and clothes on our backs. Most of the time, I had a job with health insurance. Additionally, we had a loving, supportive family and a church beside us. No, I did not do it on my own—it took a village. I am not saying everything will be perfect or have everything you want, as everyone's story will be different. There will be challenges and struggles, but you can accomplish more than you think with God on your side. Scripture tells us when we lean on Jesus, He takes our burden, "For my yoke is easy, and my burden is light" (Matthew 11:30 KJV). God never promises a bowl full of cherries! What He promises is joy, not happiness, through Jesus Christ. However, I have found happiness through the "Joy." "Now may the God of hope fill you with all joy and peace in believing, so that you will abound in hope by the power of the Holy Spirit" (Romans 15:13 NASB). Also, check out Psalms 16:11.

A message to the families and friends of those in a crisis pregnancy. Love your daughters, nieces, and such who are experiencing a crisis. You do not need to condone what they have done or how they got in that predicament, but you need to love them. Be supportive. Go to the doctor or a pro-life pregnancy care clinic with them. Most clinics offer ultrasounds, which show the development of the fetus. Depending upon your relationship, please be reminded that the child they are carrying is your grandchild, niece/nephew, or another family member, or perhaps a good friend. No, it will not be easy. My family told me they do not condone what I did, but they will stand beside me, love me, and still do, even in my sixties!

I will share that I did contemplate adoption in the early stages of the pregnancy. My parents told me they would adopt the baby if that were my decision. However, when I was nearly four months pregnant, I felt the first kick and movement and thought, *that is my baby, and I'm going to keep it!*

I did not know if my baby were a male or female, for they did not use ultrasound during that time frame because they did not know what the effects would be to the embryo or fetus. They only did ultrasounds if there was a possibility of a medical issue. So it wasn't until my baby was born that I knew I had a daughter.

I asked my daughter's permission to talk about this experience, and she said, "Yes." However, she also wanted me to add, "We all need to take personal responsibility for our actions." In other words, abortion is not the solution.

The scriptures inform us that children are a blessing from God, such as Psalms 147:13, Psalms 37:26, and Psalms 127:4–5.

> As arrows are in the hand of a mighty man; so are children of the youth. Happy is the man that hath his quiver full of them: they shall not be ashamed, but they shall speak with the enemies in the gate. (Psalms 127:4–5 KJV)

To the women who have had an abortion, there is healing available, and God does forgive. Call a local church or check the website for pro-life pregnancy care clinics, and ask for "Post-abortion" counseling, as some clinics offer this emotional healing process. Perhaps one of you will go through the therapy sessions, and after you had some time to heal, you can be an instructor yourself and help others. It is a wonderful feeling for the weight of guilt to be lifted off your shoulders—God allows U-Turns.

Along those lines, there is emotional help for the fathers as well. There is counseling available to assist the fathers dealing with the grief of losing their child through abortion, whether or not it was their choice.

God's Divine Wrath is coming to the world, and not just for killing innocent blood. The individual curse or judgment might not happen until someone is standing before God on judgment day. Whether someone believes in judgment or not is beside the point. The Bible states that everyone will be standing before God to have their deeds judged accordingly (2 Corinthians 5:10, 1 Peter 1:17).

The Bible is clear on the sanctity of life.

> This is what the LORD says, *He who is* your Redeemer, and the one who formed you from the womb: "I, the LORD, am the maker of all things, Stretching out the heavens by Myself And spreading out the earth alone." (Isaiah 44:24 NASB)

The Lord is speaking to the prophet, Jeremiah.

> "Before I formed you in the womb I knew you, And before you were born I consecrated you; I have appointed you as a prophet to the nations." (Jeremiah 1:5 NASB)

Luke 1:42–45 shares a time when Mary, carrying Jesus in her womb, visited her cousin Elisabeth, carrying John the Baptist in her womb, and said to Mary, "For behold, when the sound of your greeting reached my ears, the baby leaped in my womb for joy" (Luke 1:44 NASB)

Additional scriptural documentation for the sanctity of life:

Job 3:16, Psalms 51:5, 139:13, Isaiah 44:24, 49:1, 49:5, Jeremiah 20:15–18.

Solution: Stop the Abortions!

Overall, worldwide and as a country, we need to honor God's Word. We need to pray and stop the madness! Stop the abortions! Start honoring God by valuing life—all life! Donate to and pray for pro-life organizations, clinics, and such.[74] Write the legislative members to overturn the Roe v. Wade decision of 1973! If all Christians ban together 100% to fight abortion, no matter what political party or where they live in the world, I sincerely believe we can stop it! However, unfortunately, many Christians believe in abortion, including some churches that support it, calling it "pro-choice." We need to pray for that mindset to be overturned as well.

The help is out there if you need it. You have the right to Pro-life!

The Bible offers more than sufficient evidence that God does indeed love us! But the question is: Do we love God?

Our travels will now take us on a side trip—Jesus' descent to the lower regions of the earth. I like to describe it as a journey within a journey.

---

[74] Note: See end of book for list of resources.

CHAPTER 5

Jesus' Descent to Hades

The Descent of Christ into hell
Stock Illustration©Getty image.

Is there a Postmortem Opportunity for Salvation?
A Journey within a Journey

CHAPTER 5

Jesus' Descent to Hades

Let us take a different road and pretend we are traveling with Jesus to the lower regions of the earth. Perhaps we can learn what He was trying to teach us about the afterlife through what the Bible says about it. Further, let us review "the rich man and Lazarus story" with fresh eyes, for its message is powerful. We will now begin our journey.

Background

Before writing this account, I wanted to answer the question biblically, "Does God love us?" As I searched the scriptures and praying for answers, the Holy Spirit brought to my mind those who died before Christ died on the cross for our sins. That led me to search out further what the scriptures had to say.

Since I was in junior high, I have always believed that Jesus visited Hades in spirit form after His death on the cross to preach His gospel to those Old Testament disobedient disbelievers to give them another opportunity for salvation. I learned that this subject is very controversial, as many theologians have varying beliefs regarding the possibility of a second chance for redemption. The topic is very controversial because it also includes the idea of whether Christ descended to Hades (Sheol, hell, lower regions of the earth; Ephesians 4:4–10; 1 Peter 3:18–20) to share His gospel with those who died before His death and resurrection.

With further research, including the scripture mentioned above, I have learned that "scholars argue" and that the subject "is hotly debated by scholars."[75] So I wondered why believers argued with each other. Perhaps I am trying to simplify things too much; however, I humbly feel that the Bible says what it says and that we believe it or do not.

We must study the scriptures carefully so we can determine truthful answers to our questions. I am curious to see if my belief will change after diving into God's Word regarding postmortem opportunities for salvation.

Discussion

First, we need to look at specific Bible passages for our answers.

- Proverbs 3:5–6: We are not to lean on our own understanding.
- Isaiah 55:8–9: God's thoughts are not our thoughts.
- Luke 16:19–31: The Rich Man and Lazarus story: Is this a parable?

---

[75] "Descent into hell," *Zondervan Illustrated Bible Dictionary.* Retrieved from Biblegateway. com.

- Luke 23:43: Jesus said to one of the thieves on a cross beside Him that he would be in paradise.
- Luke 23:46: Jesus' spirit left His human body as He cried out with His last breath.
- John 3:13, 6:62, 16:28: These verses speak of Jesus' resurrection.
- Acts 2:27, 2:31: This passage explains His body will not suffer decay, nor will He be abandoned to Hades.
- Ephesians 1:20–23: God raised Jesus from the dead, and He sits at God's right hand in heaven.
- Ephesians 4:8–10: When Jesus ascended on high, He led a host of captives from the lower regions of the earth.
- Hebrews 9:27: All men are to die once and then face judgment.
- 1 Peter 3:18–20: Christ died once for all for our sins, and He went and made proclamation to the disobedient in prison (Hades).
- 1 Peter 4:5–6 (KJV): "The gospel preached also to them that are dead."
- Revelation 1:18 (KJV): This explains to us that Jesus lived, died, and now "lives for evermore" He has the "keys of hell and of death."

Who shall give account to him that is ready to judge the quick and the dead. For for this cause was the gospel preached also to them that are dead, that they might be judged according to men in the flesh, but live according to God in the spirit. (1 Peter 4:5–6 KJV)

A similar passage to consider is found in 1 Peter. Some translations state "made proclamation" instead of "preached." Here is an example.

> In which He also went and made proclamation to the spirits in prison, who once were disobedient when the patience of God kept waiting in the days of Noah, during the construction of the ark, in which a few, that is eight persons, were brought safely through *the* water. (1 Peter 3:19–20 NASB)

Gomes explained,

> Some have used this text to teach that Christ offered a postmortem opportunity of salvation for unbelievers, either to those who never heard the gospel or to those who rejected it when alive. Others see a reference to Old Testament believers, who were waiting for Christ to preach the gospel to them.[76]

Gomes made excellent references to how others believe regarding this subject. I prefer to believe the OT believers were waiting for Christ to preach His gospel and take them to heaven; however, I also believe that the OT disobedient needed to hear the same message and were offered a second chance for salvation. We will learn later in this account if this is accurate.

---

[76] See the discussion of these different views in Jobes, *1 Peter,* 270; Simon E. Kistemaker, *Exposition of James, Epistles of John, Peter, and Jude,* NTC (Grand Rapids: Baker, 2002), 163–164, quoted in Alan W. Gomes, *40 Questions About Heaven and Hell*, 358.

The Rich Man and Lazarus (Luke 16), published in 1860
Stock Illustration©Getty image.

Side Trip: Is the Rich Man and Lazarus Story a Parable?

Is the story of the rich man and Lazarus in Luke 16:19–31 a parable? While researching online, reading books, and asking various knowledgeable individuals, I learned that the "story of the rich man and Lazarus" may or may not be a parable. Kenneth Berding disagreed with me "that the rich man and Lazarus story can be used to draw out details about the afterlife. It is a parable that makes a main point. You have to be careful with parables not to make them say too much."[77]

In the interest of being theologically correct, I thought about and highly valued Berding's comments; however, I was not in agreement with him. I did not know exactly why at the time, except that I kept thinking there were too many details to ignore in that story and that it seemed to me to be more than just a parable.

I do not want to leave the impression that I am discounting Jesus' parables because they are vital in assisting unbelievers (outsiders) to understand the biblical theology Jesus was trying to teach (Matthew 13:10–13). The Word of God is full of other stories and actual accounts that we learn from; we learn theology in many ways, not only with parables.

I decided to call my brother Peter because he has studied the Bible with great effort most of his life and has an excellent knowledge of God's Word. We have had many theological discussions throughout our lives, and I wanted to hear his thoughts on the subject. I explained the comments on parables to him, and he agreed that the rich man and Lazarus story might not be a parable. He said he had four main reasons he thought that.

- **Reason 1.** Almost all the stories that are parables announce at their beginnings that they are parables. The story of the rich man and Lazarus is not designated as a parable.
- **Reason 2.** In the parables, Jesus does not use names for any of the characters in them. In the story of the rich

____

[77] Kenneth Berding, email dialogue February 20, 2020.

man and Lazarus, except for the rich man, names such as Abraham, Lazarus, and Moses are used.

- **Reason 3.** In the parables, Jesus used examples from daily life that people could relate to and understand. Jesus also used common phrases and items such as vineyards and talents (gold). However, in the story of the rich man and Lazarus, Jesus did not do this. Instead, He used biblical terminology such as Hades. In addition, he detailed images of things never seen or experienced, such as a "great chasm has been fixed" (ESV), or "gulf" (KJV), "Abraham's bosom" (KJV), and as the Rich Man stated, "for I am tormented in this flame" (KJV).
- **Reason 4.** In no other parable does Jesus refer to the scriptures, yet only in this one does He mention "Moses and the Prophets," which is used throughout the Gospels to refer to the scriptures.
  - ✓ Luke 24:23, 24:44, John 1:45, Acts 26:22, 28:23

I also searched for "parables" on Biblegateway.com, viewing five different translations: NASB, NIV, ESV, KJV, and NKJV; however, the rich man and Lazarus story did not come up as a parable in the list of scriptures. Yet, when I chose NLT, it was listed as a parable.

While on Biblegateway.com, I decided to view one of the Bible dictionaries available, *Zondervan*'s. I read the definition of Abraham's bosom (side): "A figure of speech used by Jesus in the parable of Lazarus and the rich man."[78] I was surprised to see that *Zondervan's Dictionary* had stated it was a parable;

---

[78] "Abraham's Bosom (side)," *Zondervan's Illustrated Bible Dictionary.* Retrieved from Biblegateway.com.

however, it did not negate the possibility of not being a parable because of the four reasons my brother had given me and the other information I found on Biblegateway.com.

Additionally, there is truth in the rich man and Lazarus story. It reads, "the captives," Abraham's bosom side, which corresponds to this.

> When he ascended on high, he took many captives and gave gifts to his people. (Ephesians 4:8 NIV)

There are far too many details in the rich man and Lazarus story that Jesus stated compared to the parables and bearing in mind the four reasons my brother mentioned. Therefore, this story should not be considered a parable.

I know many theologians debate about this story being a parable or not. After I had given a sneak peek of Chapter 5 to my former high school friend, Stephen Raines, he replied with the following.

> Thanks for the sneak preview of Chapter Five. You've been doing your homework. For a "non-theologian," your digging is impressive. I especially appreciated your taking the time to assert that Luke's "Rich Man and Lazarus" passage is not a parable. I am reminded of the adage saying, "for every mile of road, there's often two miles of ditch—one on either side." Looking forward to seeing the finished book!

In the balance of this account, you will soon discover just how much detail is in Jesus' story of the rich man and Lazarus.

I know it appears that I am elevating my brother's reasons over that of scholars; however, we must weigh my brother's reasons versus *Zondervan*'s and Berding's comments. Even though the NLT stated this passage was a parable, the other four translations did not.

For this theological account, I am taking the position that the rich man and Lazarus story is not a parable but was included explicitly in the Bible to help us understand the decisions we make now will affect our afterlife status. When we link this story with other scripture, we can better understand Jesus' descent to Hades.

My brother and I are not saying it is indeed not a parable or that we do not respect the theological comments of those holding degrees in theology. We believe that the rich man and Lazarus story is not a parable; perhaps it is in a class by itself. Nevertheless, I feel that this subject should be theologically reconsidered and researched.

Discussion Continued

Second, we need to look at and understand God and who He is. The following are just a few of His awesome attributes.

- He created the heavens and the earth (Genesis 1:1; Job 38:4).
- He is omnipresent (Psalms 139:7–10; Colossians 1:17).
- He is sovereign (Psalms 139; Ezekiel 18:3–4; Romans 11:33; Revelation 21:6).

- He is all-powerful (Genesis 19:24; Job 37:23).
- He is a triune God (2 Corinthians 13:14).
- He is also known as Elohim (Hebrew), a plural God (Genesis 1:1, 1:26).
- He is full of grace, mercy, and lovingkindness (Psalms 86:15).
- He is holy and righteous (Psalms 99:9, 145:17).
- He is a God of justice and judgment (Deuteronomy 32:4; 2 Thessalonians 2:10–13).

Why do we want to put limits or conditions on what God can or cannot do? Our human minds cannot even fathom infinity for one New York nanosecond; we can understand only finite things. We are born, we live, and we die. When we die a physical death, our bodies go to dust, yet our souls are eternal—our souls will reunite with our resurrected bodies during the resurrection.

> And many of them that sleep in the dust of the earth shall awake, some to everlasting life, and some to shame and everlasting contempt. (Daniel 12:2 KJV)

> And shall come forth; they that have done good, into the resurrection of life; and they that have done evil, unto the resurrection of damnation. (John 5:29 KJV)

Believers are blessed "to be absent from the body and to be present with the Lord" (2 Corinthians 5:8 KJV). If we are unbelievers, we wait for judgment.

Sadly, unbelievers' deaths mean separation from the body until their bodies' resurrection, as discussed above, and separation from the Lord eternally (2 Thessalonians 1:8–9). This separation from God means suffering conscious torment, along with "their fire is not extinguished" (Mark 9:48, NASB).

In Luke 16:24 (KJV), the rich man claims, "… for I am tormented in this flame." Matthew explained it further.

> So shall it be at the end of the world: the angels shall come forth, and sever the wicked from among the just, And shall cast them into the furnace of fire: there shall be wailing and gnashing of teeth. (Matthew 13:49–50 KJV)

✓ Additional Biblical reference: Matthew 22:11–13

This explanation shows us that the lake of fire is not complete annihilation; if so, everyone would be dead and therefore silent. This passage is one of the saddest in the Bible.

> In flaming fire taking vengeance on them that know not God, and that obey not the gospel of our Lord Jesus Christ: Who shall be punished with everlasting destruction from the presence of the Lord, and from the glory of his power. (2 Thessalonians 1:8–9 KJV)

This description of the lake of fire is not conducive to any way, shape, or form for a purification process leading anyone to reconcile with God. The scripture further describes that those persons will be "away from the presence of the Lord and from the glory of his power." How can someone reconcile with God when He and His glory is absent? And the passage says, "everlasting destruction," which indicates ongoing destruction, not purification, which further counteracts the concept of complete annihilation.

Robert Peterson, an advocate for traditionalism and coauthor of *Two Views of Hell*, explained it this way.

> In contrast, Fudge believes that when human beings die, no immaterial part (soul or spirit) survives. Instead, the whole person expires and ceases to exist until the resurrection. I refute this unbiblical notion on pages 171–174, where I pointed to six passages that teach that death is the separation of our material and immaterial parts and that our soul or spirit departs from the body at death.[79]

The six passages Peterson used below come from the NIV.

> For believers, death means being "away from the body and at home with the Lord (2 Cor. 5:8). That is why our Lord said at his death, "Father, into your hands I commit my spirit" (Luke 23:46). That is why he promised the penitent dying thief, "Today you will be with me in paradise" (Lk. 23:43). That is why Paul described departing the body to be with Christ as "better by far" than remaining in the body (Phil. 1:23). And that is why scripture speaks of deceased human beings as

---

[79] Fudge, *Two Views of Hell*, 87.

souls "under the altar" (Rev. 6:9) and as "spirits as righteous men made perfect" (Heb. 12:23).[80]

As a reminder, Edward Fudge is an advocate for Conditionalism and coauthor of *Two Views of Hell.*

Additionally, some may conclude or argue that Jesus could not have descended to Hades because of the following verses.

> Because you will not abandon my soul to Hades, nor allow your Holy One to undergo decay. (Acts 2:27 NASB)

> He looked ahead and spoke of the resurrection of the Christ, that He was neither abandoned to Hades, nor did His flesh suffer decay. (Acts 2:31 NASB)

I agree that Jesus' body would not have suffered decay because His body was in a borrowed tomb—temporarily—as we will soon learn and His visit to Hades was temporary. He is who He is. His spirit descended to Hades, and because of who He is, there would be no harm—decay or abandonment. He is the almighty God, the Prince of Peace, and the King of Kings to briefly describe Him. Further, before His body was crucified, He was transfigured (Matthew 17:1–10). I believe this caused positive benefits to His body for him to endure what He needed to accomplish.

Jesus' spirit descended after His body died on the cross. He was in spirit form, not physical form. His human body was in

---

[80] Fudge, *Two Views of Hell,* 171.

the tomb. Luke 23:46 (ESV) tells us He breathed His last breath after committing His Spirit to His Father.

✓ Similar verses are Matthew 27:50 and Mark 15:37

People forget that God is omnipotent; He can do whatever He wants; it is not for us to question His sovereignty. God asked Job, "Where were you when I laid the foundation of the earth? Tell me if you have understanding" (Job 38:4 NASB). I am not trying to paint an ugly picture of God; however, I feel we get things mixed up. He is God, and we are man. People seem to devalue God and think He should do things their way. The scriptures remind us, "'For My thoughts are not your thoughts, Nor are your ways My ways,' declares the LORD." (Isaiah 55:8 NASB) and "Do not lean on your own understanding" (Proverbs 3:5b NASB).

I take the position that Christ "preached" (KJV), "made proclamation" (NASB) to all the inhabitants in both regions. In Luke 16:19–31, regarding the rich man and Lazarus, we learn that there are two regions with a "great chasm has been fixed" (ESV), "gulf" (KJV) between them, and neither side can cross over (v. 26) "in the lower earthly regions" (Ephesians 4:9 NIV).

The region where the rich man was "is conceived as an underground prison with locked gates to which Christ holds the key."[81]

✓ Taken from Revelation 1:18 KJV

These souls are the disobedient imprisoned spirits. This lower region is also known as—hell, Hades, or Sheol—not

---

[81] "Hades," Mounce, *Complete Expository Dictionary*, found through BibleGateway.com.

the lake of fire. This region is a temporary place because hell (Hades/Sheol) will be thrown into the lake of fire (Revelation 20:14). On this side, the souls are in "agony" (Luke 16:24, NASB; the KJV version reads, "I am tormented").

Abraham's bosom side is a different area in which the souls are not in torment and are considered OT believers, as noted earlier by Gomes. The souls that are in this area are also known as captives.

The rich man and Abraham were having a conversation. According to scripture, either side could not cross over, but they were communicating. There would be no dialogue between those in heaven and those in the lake of fire. Therefore, this lower region is a temporary place. Additionally, Abraham's bosom side will no longer be in the lower regions of the earth because Jesus takes the captives with Him, as you will read in the conclusion of this chapter.

Since Jesus died on the cross for humanity's sins, we are now in a state of grace and no longer under the law. There will no longer be any additions to Abraham's bosom side because, as Apostle Paul told us, "We are confident, I say, and willing rather to be absent from the body, and to be present with the Lord" (2 Corinthians 5:8 KJV). Paul also shares with us in Philippians 1:23 (NASB), "But I am hard-pressed from both *directions*, having the desire to depart and be with Christ, for *that* is very much better." In keeping with scripture, the souls in Hades will continue to reside there along with new inhabitants until Judgment Day; "And death and hell were cast into the lake of fire. This is the second death" (Revelation 20:14 KJV).

Now that I have laid out biblical facts and groundwork, I will attempt to explain the relevance of Jesus' descent to Hades.

My Perspective of Jesus' Descent to Hades

Jesus was in spirit form. His spirit left His human body after His death on the cross (Luke 23:46). Because of who He is, He could descend to the lower regions of the earth (Hades). During His visit, He preached (made proclamation) to all the souls in this lower region. Scripture tells us of the timing of Jesus' death—Jesus died around the ninth hour (3:00 p.m. Luke 23:44 NLT). Thus, the timing of Jesus' death will soon be relevant.

The controversial issue of whether Jesus descended to Hades or not has been debated. In his book, Gomes referenced the following passage from Luke 23:43 to explain, "Christ's immaterial spirit did not descent into hades but instead went directly to paradise."[82] I disagree with that interpretation because the scripture states, "today you will be with Me in paradise" (Luke 23:43 NASB). Today does not mean directly, nor does it mean immediately; it means today. The spirit of the penitent thief would ascend directly to heaven; however, Jesus' spirit descended to Hades to preach (made proclamation) according to scripture (1 Peter 4:5–6), as noted earlier in this chapter. Scripture does not tell us how long Jesus was visiting Hades. Yet it is reasonable to ascertain that He finished what He needed to accomplish, and then He ascended to heaven on the same day. Per scripture, His spirit left his physical body around 3:00 p.m.; thus, He had until midnight to preach His gospel to the souls of the lower regions. Jesus then ascended to heaven in keeping with the truth of the scriptures "today you will be with me in paradise" (Luke 23:43 NLT).

---

[82] Gomes, *40 Questions,* 74.

There is a far better reasonable interpretation that Jesus did not ascend directly (immediately) to heaven with the repentant thief because He was omnipresent in spirit form. While Jesus was on earth, He was not omnipresent. Scripture tells us he walked or took a boat to where he needed to travel—He even walked on water! (Matthew 14:25–27).

Because of who He is, no harm would come to Him. I believe He did this willingly for the reason of who He is.

- He came from heaven in human form to understand us and what we go through.
- While in the desert for forty days, He was tempted by the devil, just as we are tempted (Luke 4:1–13).
- He felt hunger (Luke 4:2 ESV), "he was hungry."
- He wept (John 11:35, regarding the death and resurrection of His friend, Lazarus, whom He loved. KJV, "Jesus wept").
- He felt compassion for people.
  - For the inhabitants of Nineveh (Jonah 4:11)
  - In Matthew 9:36–38, Jesus shared with His disciples that He felt compassion for the people and said, the "harvest is plentiful, but the workers are few" (NASB)
  - For the crowd He preached to—He fed the five thousand (Matthew 14)

By going to the lower regions, He would understand the torment and agony of the souls who had rejected God/Him. His heart and soul must have been grieved. He wanted to save everyone; that is why He died on the cross. The free-will choice is in our hands. The decision is ours and ours alone.

Because the rich man and Abraham could communicate, Jesus had that capability too because of who He is. During Jesus' visit, He preaches His gospel and proclaims His fulfillment of the OT prophecy about Himself, such as but not limited to Isaiah 9:6, 53, 55:1–7 and Luke 24:44.

Another factor to consider, after Jesus rose from the dead, He was seen by over 500 people before ascending to heaven to sit at the right hand of God (1 Corinthians 15: 4–10). My understanding about this is He did not do that on the day His spirit left His body. Instead, for a few days (Acts 13:31 NASB) or a few months, Jesus showed himself intermittently to others before ascending to heaven on a cloud (Acts 1:9). Again, I believe Jesus could not have done this unless He was omnipresent.

Something to look forward to—The return of Jesus. As Christians, we are to wait for Him eagerly.

> Dear friends, we are already God's children, but he has not yet shown us what we will be like when Christ appears. But we do know that we will be like him, for we will see him as he really is. And all who have this eager expectation will keep themselves pure, just as he is pure. (1 John 3:2–3 NLT)

> And, Jesus will be returning for us on a cloud (Acts 1:11).

What about Those Who Have Not Heard the Gospel?

I want to address some concerns about those who may not have heard about salvation. What about those who have not heard or read John 3:16 or anything close to it? God's Word covers this.

> For since the creation of the world His invisible *attributes, that is*, His eternal power and divine nature, have been clearly perceived, being understood by what has been made, so that they are without excuse. (Romans 1:20 NASB)

> ✓ Also, read Job 12: 7–9; Psalms 19:1–6; Jeremiah 5:21–31; Romans 1

We all need to understand that God gives everyone knowledge about himself through his creation, as described in Romans 1:20, and we will be held accountable for that knowledge. To further explain this, Gomes added this quote from his book, *40 Questions,* from another author, Henry W. Holloman.

> Even if one is without direct knowledge of God's will and law, God can equally judge thought, word and deed in light of the individual's natural sense

of right and wrong (Ezek 7:3, 27; 24:14; Mt 7:2; Lk 12:46–48; Rom 2:1, 14–15; Jas 3:1).[83]

Gomes further describes the "light" that we are given.

> Everyone will be judged based upon what they do with the light that they have. Those who have no special revelation from God nevertheless have the light of conscience and creation, and God will punish them for violating that light.[84]

> Greater light carries with it greater responsibility, together with more severe punishment for repudiating that light.[85]

Scripture also assures us that God does reach out to all persons, past, present, and future, who may not have directly heard of the gospel, whether in writing or verbally.
Jesus said,

> Behold, I stand at the door and knock; if anyone hears My voice and opens the door, I will come in to him and will dine with him, and he with Me. (Revelation 3:20 NASB)

In the OT, God assures us,

---

[83] Henry W. Holloman, "Judgment," *Kregel Dictionary of the Bible and Theology* (Grand Rapids: Kregel, 2005), 263, quoted in Alan W. Gomes, *40 Questions about Heaven and Hell* (Grand Rapids: Kregel Academics,2018), 152.

[84] Gomes, *40 Questions*, 173.

[85] Gomes, *40 Questions*, 173.

I love all who love me. Those who search will
surely find me. (Proverbs 8:17 NLT)

Isn't this magnificent? Jesus will reach out to "anyone,"
whether on the highest mountain or in the deepest jungle. It
may not be in the form you and I would expect, but He will
make himself known to all. Yet, it is the individual's independent
decision to open the door of their heart and allow Jesus in to
receive eternal life ("whosoever believeth" John 3:16 KJV).

What About Those Who Died Before Christ Came to Die for Our Sins

The souls of the dead who rejected God before their death
and Christ died for our sins do not receive a postmortem
opportunity for salvation. Jesus shared His gospel to the two
regions' inhabitants, but He did not offer a second opportunity for
redemption. Instead, Jesus' message was that He had fulfilled
not only the OT prophecy about Himself but also "to proclaim
his victory through the cross and upcoming resurrection."[86]

Once our human bodies die, there are no second chances
for our souls; we are without excuse (Romans 1:20). If the
disobedient dead souls in this lower region get a second
opportunity, all who die should get second chances, but we
know that that is not the case through scripture.

In Luke 16:16–31 (KJV), the rich man asked if Lazarus
could give him a drop of water on his tongue, and Abraham
said no (vv. 24 & 25). Then (vv. 28 & 29), he asked if Lazarus
could be sent to his father's house, for he had five brothers he

---

[86] Berding, email dialogue, February 20, 2020.

wanted to be warned. Abraham answered the rich man, "They have Moses and the prophets; let them hear them."

In 1 Peter 3:19–20, Peter wrote that these "spirits in prison" (v19 NASB), when alive in their bodies in the days of Noah, had heard the truth through Noah but had rejected it; they were without excuse. Therefore, there are no postmortem opportunities for salvation.

I want to point out an additional piece of proof that there is no postmortem opportunity for salvation. The disobedient who died know there are no second chances for redemption. The rich man asked for a drop of water and for his brothers to be warned; he did not ask for a second chance because he knew where he was and why. Abraham told him there was a gulf between them, and no one on either side could cross; this clarifies that a person's soul's destination is set upon death.

Through scripture, we know that both sides are temporary until Jesus' visit. The imprisoned rebellious spirits were awaiting judgment, but the captives, Abraham's bosom side, would not be staying there.

A Beautiful End to Christ's Visit to Hades

The end of Jesus' descent to Hades is *beautiful* because He takes the captives away with Him to Heaven. Scripture states, "When he ascended on high, he took many captives and gave gifts to his people" (Ephesians 4:8 NIV). Just imagine if we were there looking upon this beautiful event—all the OT believers floating up with Jesus to spend eternity with Him in heaven—Oh, what a glorious sight!

Conclusion for Jesus' Descent to Hades

Jesus "finished" three tasks: dying on the cross as the final perfect sacrificial Lamb of God to be a ransom for all humanity, to preach His Gospel to the inhabitants of the lower regions of the earth, and take the captives back with Him to heaven. Therefore, Jesus would be in paradise "today" as per scripture.

Those who reject God have no postmortem opportunities for salvation. I knew that for current and future souls, but I had always thought those imprisoned souls had another chance for redemption. Berding reminded me of the following verse.[87]

> And just as it is destined for people to die once, and
> after this *comes* judgment. (Hebrews 9:27 NASB)

Now I know there are no postmortem opportunities for salvation for sure, and no one is without excuse.

To Sum Up Chapter 5

We all are given light about creation, a sense of right and wrong, and what God's invisible attributes show us, and we will be held accountable for that light.

While researching the subject of light, I came across some additional scripture that might be of interest.

- Psalms 92:11, 119:130
- Proverbs 29:13
- Isaiah 5:20

---

[87] Berding, email dialogue, February 20, 2020.

- Matthew 6:22–23
- Mark 4:22
- Luke 11:35
- Ephesians 5:7–10

We have an opportunity for salvation while we are alive, whether through Noah, Moses, any of the prophets, including the light given to us, or direct knowledge of Jesus Christ.

The OT disobedient were given the same opportunity as the OT believers in Abraham's bosom before their death in Noah's and Moses' days. Just as it is since Jesus came to die for our sins, we all have the same opportunity for salvation. I understand that parts of our world are where the inhabitants do not have access to a Bible in their language or missionaries to explain the gospel. However, according to Romans 1:20, they are without excuse. It is just a matter of personal choice.

Does God Love Us?

Yes, He does. He sent His Son to die on the cross to save us from the lake of fire. He loves all people and allows them to choose Him of their own free will. In God's eyes—all humanity matters! Everyone is responsible for their soul's destination. He knows our hearts, no matter where we are in our lives.

- Psalms 44:21 (NASB): "For He knows the secrets of the heart."
- Psalms 139:2 (NASB): "You understand my thought from far away."

- Jeremiah 17:10 (NASB): "I, the LORD, search the heart, I test the mind, To give to each person according to his ways, According to the results of his deeds."

We must act before our death. We must believe in Jesus Christ as our Lord and Savior—There is no other way.
We read of God's love for us in John 3:16 (KJV).

> For God so loved the world that He gave His only begotten Son, that whosoever believeth in Him should not perish, but have everlasting life.

> John 14:6 (KJV) explains that the only way to the Father is through Jesus.

> Jesus saith unto him, I am the way, the truth, and the life: no man cometh unto the Father, but by me.

Believers will have eternal life with Him in heaven, while unbelievers will have an eternal judgment in the lake of fire.

> Depart from me, accursed people, into the eternal fire which has been prepared for the devil and his angels. (Matthew 25:41 NASB)

> "… but the righteous into eternal life." (Matthew 25:46 NASB)

Thank you for taking this journey within a journey with me.

The next stop is the conclusion, which answers several questions and addresses some concerns mentioned earlier in our journey.

PART THREE

A Biblical Overview of Eternity— With or Without God

IN CONCLUSION

A Soul's Destination

The End is Not the End
Heaven or Hell? Your Choice!

IN CONCLUSION—A SOUL'S DESTINATION

The End Is Not the End

We searched the scriptures together to find out what the Bible says regarding death and eternity for our souls, and we found the following.

- For believers and unbelievers, death is not final.
- For unbelievers, the second death is not the final death of their bodies and souls. As defined in the Bible, the second death is a final destination of one's being (body and soul) into the lake of fire. (Revelation 20:15, 21:8)
- Revelation 2:11 assures believers that the second death will not hurt them.

Is Death Final?

The only final thing is the eternal destination of one's soul—heaven or the lake of fire (Daniel 12:2; Matthew 13:41–42, 25:31–46, John 5:29 and Revelation 20:14–15).

When people take their last breaths, their souls' eternal destination is determined by their relationship with Jesus

Christ—Are their names in the Book of Life? (Revelation 20:15, 21:27).

I have heard many say that there is no lake of fire and ask how a loving God full of grace and mercy could torment people for eternity. Let us review what we have learned: three critical spiritual factors to consider to answer that question.

1. Condemnation of humankind—original sin in the Garden of Eden
2. The offer of salvation—the redemption of our sins through Jesus Christ
3. Humanity's rejection of salvation—past, present, and future

Adam and Eve sinned in the Garden of Eden by disobeying God and His instructions (Genesis 2:17) not to eat from the Tree of the Knowledge of Good and Evil. Since then, humanity has been under condemnation (Genesis 3:17–19). Further, scriptures tell us:

> For God sent not his Son into the world to condemn the world; but that the world through him might be saved. He that believeth on him is not condemned: but he that believeth not is condemned already, because he hath not believed in the name of the only begotten Son of God. (John 3:17–18 KJV)

Scripture describes unbelief and its consequences.

"Then He will also say to those on His left, 'Depart from Me, you accursed people, into the eternal fire which has been prepared for the devil and his angels;'" (Matthew 25:41 NASB)

For since the creation of the world His invisible *attributes, that is*, His eternal power and divine nature, have been clearly perceived, being understood by what has been made, so that they are without excuse. (Romans 1:20 NASB)

✓ Romans 1:18–32 defines penalties of unbelief.

This is another powerful verse.

But if a righteous person turns from their righteousness and commits sin and does the same detestable things the wicked person does, will they live? None of the righteous things that person has done will be remembered. Because of the unfaithfulness they are guilty of and because of the sins they have committed, they will die. (Ezekiel 18:24 NIV)

Do not be dismayed.

For God has not destined us for wrath, but for obtaining salvation through our Lord Jesus Christ. (1 Thessalonians 5:9 NASB)

As I shared with you in Chapter 3, the Books of Lamentations and Ezekiel expressed, God takes no pleasure in His wrath and does not afflict willingly. Therefore, we are saved only through accepting His Son, Jesus Christ.

Other Philosophies and Beliefs

This area is sensitive because many strongly believe what they believe. However, man-derived philosophies are not the theology of the Bible. Intellectually we all know the Bible cannot teach three views of hell, or the Bible would be a work of fiction. The Bible teaches one view of the lake of fire: thus, making two views unscriptural.

The non-Biblical beliefs are dangerous because they deter people from seeking the almighty God. Most importantly, they diminish and devalue what Jesus did on the cross and further diminishes the magnitude of sin. If there were no lake of fire with eternal judgment, there would have been no need for God to save us through Jesus Christ.

People reject God and His judgment because they do not want to accept His judgment. They refuse His judgment and justice, which is His wrath of the lake of fire. People want to live the way they want to live by their will, not God's will. People refuse to submit to God's ways, and they do not want to be judged for how they live.

People develop and encourage various philosophies and belief systems because they will not accept God's judgment or its consequences. As a result, some believers and unbelievers have a limited perspective on what Jesus did on the cross. Further, I understand that some will disagree with me on this.

Some people are not sure of their salvation or perhaps do not believe in redemption. Maybe it is more comfortable for them to deal with the thought that they will either just die or go through a purification process and not be eternally punished in a lake of fire at the end of their lives. If only people would read the Bible and believe what it says about salvation and how God assures us, perhaps they would accept with confidence the assurance of eternity in heaven.

Burk, one of the contributing authors of *Four Views On Hell*, courageously stated the following.

> Our emotional reflex against the traditional doctrine of hell reveals what we really believe about God. We tend to have a diminished view of sin—and thus of the judgment due to sin—because we have a diminished view of God. The god of our imagination sometimes fall short of the God of scripture. We fail to take sin and judgment as seriously as we ought because we fail to take God as seriously as we ought. And so we are often tempted to view the penalty of hell—eternal conscious suffering under the wrath of God—as an overreaction on God's part.[88]

Burk hit the spiritual nail on the head. I agree with Burk on his theology of who God is. I am not trying to point any fingers at any person or belief system, and I certainly do not want to offend anyone. However, I want to stress that we seem to think we know who God is and how judgment should be administered. We may not always understand everything in His

---

[88] Sprinkle, *Four Views On Hell*, 20.

Word, but it is clear about God's love and His judgment; we just need to believe it.

We get our beliefs from the Bible. In other words, we read the Word of God to see what the Bible says; we do not search the scriptures to find passages to try to prove our beliefs. As I have shown throughout this book, you were offered the "truth" when other scriptures were correlated, primarily when you evaluated the operative words. Therefore, when one takes a single passage to prove a theological statement, it can be considered a misnomer to the actual truth of what the scriptures are telling us.

Misunderstanding Scripture

An additional example of misunderstanding scripture is that some people believe that Jesus is a created being, and therefore, there is no triune God. Some base this theory on the following verse.

> He is the image of the invisible God, the firstborn
> of all creation. (Colossians 1:15 ESV)

Jesus is the firstborn, but not in our sense of understanding. He always was in spiritual form before He was physically born as a baby boy from the virgin Mary, and, therefore, the Son of God and the son of man—He was the first and only one to meet that description. Further, when you evaluate the immediate surrounding scripture, you discover a different meaning, such as the "Preeminence of Christ" (ESV) and "The Supremacy of the Son of God" (NIV), not a created being.

For by him all things were created, in heaven and on earth, visible and invisible, whether thrones or dominions or rulers or authorities—all things were created through him and for him. And he is before all things, and in him all things hold together. (Colossians 1:16–17 ESV)

Further, when you link other scriptures, you will realize that He is not a created being because scripture establishes His deity—Christ the Eternal Word (NLT).

In the beginning the Word already existed. The Word was with God, and the Word was God. He existed in the beginning with God. God created everything through him, and nothing was created except through him. The Word gave life to everything that was created, and his life brought light to everyone. The light shines in the darkness, and the darkness can never extinguish it. (John 1:1–5 NLT)

Additionally, Hebrews 1:1–3 identifies God's final word in His Son, specifically verse 2:

Hath in these last days spoken unto us by his Son, whom he hath appointed heir of all things, by whom also he made the worlds. (Hebrews 1:2 KJV)

After reading the above scriptural references, it makes another aspect clear. If Jesus was created, then how can He create things *in the beginning* with God? Something cannot create itself; someone else would have to create it. Since scripture tells us, "nothing was created except through him" (John 1:3 NLT), then Jesus already had to be with God in the beginning and during creation to make the scripture accurate—Jesus was not created. Don't forget the Holy Spirit—He was there too! The Bible does teach us our God is a Triune God: God the Father, God the Son, and God the Holy Spirit! Halleluiah! Amen!

I understand that the Bible can seem harsh and unbelievable; therefore, some people want to *soften* the scriptures with alternative beliefs. I know it is difficult to believe in an eternal fire, yet relatively easy to believe in an eternal life with God. The Bible describes both places as an eternal destination, yet we seem to interpret that heaven is real, but hell is metaphorical. If hell is symbolic, then heaven needs to be symbolic as well. God's Holy Word states both heaven and hell are eternal.

If the lake of fire was not an eternal fire, why were the demons afraid to go there? Luke 8:27–35 tells us about a true story of a man possessed by many demons. Jesus was visiting the town of this man. Jesus asked the man what his name was, and he answered: "legion" (Luke 8:30 NIV). (Note: Legion means several thousand.) "And they begged Jesus repeatedly not to order them to go into the Abyss" (Luke 8:31 NIV). Abyss is another name for the bottomless pit and the lake of fire, as discussed in Chapter 3. If the Abyss was only mere death or a purification process, then why were the demons afraid of it?

You will need to remember that those demons were once angels in the glory of heaven before Lucifer (now Satan), and they were thrown out of heaven—they know who Jesus is— they know of His power and might. Lucifer and the demons not only knew about heaven, but they knew about the truth of the lake of fire: "Even the demons believe—and shudder!" (James 2:19b ESV)

A "Diminished" Perception

The following is my explanation of a diminished perception. I am reminded of a passage that shows us the spiritually deep-rooted significance of what Jesus did on the cross. The passage is from 2 Corinthians 12:7–9 (NASB). Apostle Paul was suffering a medical or physical ailment that he called a "thorn in the flesh" (v7). Throughout my life, I have heard sermons and have spoken to others regarding Paul's issues. For example, he might have suffered from a possible facial disfigurement of some type or perhaps an eye-sight issue. The scripture is not clear on the exact ailment; however, there are different interpretations.

My focus is not specifically on the precise issue, except that Paul's challenge was something he dealt with daily. Acts 14:19 explains that Paul was stoned and left for dead; therefore, an interpretation is that it left him facially scarred. Additionally, 2 Corinthians 11:22–33 describes various beatings and imprisonments that Paul suffered. Galatians 4:13–15 also discusses Paul's "bodily illness" (NASB). Paul "pleaded with the Lord three times" (2 Corinthians 12:8 NASB) to heal him, and Jesus' response was, "My grace is sufficient for you" (2 Corinthians 12:9a NASB). Paul shares his concerns and request in the following scripture.

> And lest I should be exalted above measure
> through the abundance of the revelations,

there was given to me a thorn in the flesh, the messenger of Satan to buffet me, lest I should be exalted above measure. For this thing I besought the Lord thrice, that it might depart from me. And he said unto me, My grace is sufficient for thee: for my strength is made perfect in weakness. Most gladly therefore will I rather glory in my infirmities, that the power of Christ may rest upon me. (2 Corinthians 12:7–9 KJV)

Now, I will link the significance of what Jesus did on the cross: Jesus died to save us from eternal punishment in an everlasting fire, which is far worse than any physical, medical, or other ailments we may be suffering from temporarily here on earth. Remember, the world is a temporary place until one of two things happens. We die a physical death, or the rapture happens during our physical life. For Christians who die before the rapture, we will be present with the Lord. Those who are brought up in the rapture will be present with the Lord.

However, unbelievers who die a physical death will wait for the judgment of the lake of fire and never be with the Lord. The magnitude of God's grace is shown through His Son, Jesus Christ, by His sacrifice on the cross—because He loves us dearly (John 3:16 and John 16:27 (NLT). Some people have a limited perspective of God's saving grace because they do not understand that God's grace is powerful and saves lives for eternity!

I have often thought about God's grace in this passage, and each time I seem to grow in my understanding of its meaning spiritually. Nevertheless, I am not sure we will fully understand God's Grace and its great significance until we arrive in heaven.

I will summarize what I have learned, and my apologies if it sounds harsh; however, it is a Biblical and spiritual reality check. Belief in anything other than eternal punishment in the eternal fire, for unbelievers, shows a diminished perspective of the seriousness of sin. And, therefore, a diminished view of what Jesus did on the cross. If there was no eternal punishment for our unforgiven sin (rejecting God, i.e., blasphemy of the Holy Spirit), then Jesus died in vain.

Without the gift of salvation through Jesus Christ, which gives us the reward of eternal life in heaven, our soul's destination is eternal punishment in the lake of fire. Jesus died so that we would have eternal life and be saved from the eternal lake of fire. It is a matter of how much value, credence, and importance we put on what Jesus did on the cross. That is the core difference between traditionalism and all other perspectives regarding the fate of unbelievers.

Our God would not have sent His only begotten Son (John 3:16) to die a horrible death (John 19:1–20) if there were no eternal lake of fire. Therefore, we need to take the salvation we are offered seriously and share it with the world!

Spreading The Word

Christians are responsible for spreading the gospel of Jesus Christ even at the risk of offending someone. But, unfortunately, some casually walk through life not sharing God's message to others because they are afraid of offending them. However, I think it is worth the risk of offending someone when you consider the unbeliever's soul's destination in the eternal fire. Each person is held accountable, and they are without excuse according to Romans 1:20 whether someone shares the gospel with them or not. However, it is still the Christian's role to be obedient and follow the Great Commission.

Additionally, as believers, we are to present the gospel accurately and lovingly. We do not take responsibility for the unbeliever's response, yet we are held accountable for how we deliver the message.

> But is now made manifest by the appearing of our Saviour Jesus Christ, who hath abolished death, and hath brought life and immortality to light through the gospel: (2 Timothy 1:10 KJV)

> Matthew and Mark explain our responsibility in the Great Commission.

> And He said to them, "Go into all the world and preach the gospel to all creation. (Mark 16:15 NASB)

> Go, therefore, and make disciples of all the nations, baptizing them in the name of the Father and the Son and the Holy Spirit. (Matthew 28:19 NASB)

It is challenging to be a Christian in this world. No matter what, we must put God first, even at the cost of others or things in our life. I believe the following passage says it best.

> And everyone who has left houses or brothers
> or sisters or father or mother or children or farms
> on account of My name, will receive many times
> as much, and will inherit eternal life. (Matthew
> 19:29 NASB)

We need to be careful with this verse. It does not mean we should go out and abandon our children or spouses to serve the Lord. Yet if you recall, the fishermen Jesus called to be His disciples, along with others He called, left everything, and followed Him (Matthew 4:19, 8:21–22, Mark 1:17). If you feel God is calling you to serve Him full-time, I encourage you to seek a pastor, a Christian professor/counselor to discuss your ministry plans.

As a final note on spreading the word, we offer the world something beautiful, and that is why we must follow Jesus' command of the Great Commission.

> For we are a fragrance of Christ to God among
> those who are being saved and among those
> who are perishing. (2 Corinthians 2:15 NASB)

Does the Bible Lie or Contradict Itself?

I have shown you through scripture what Jesus said in the Word of God. We take the scripture in faith and trust indeed. What do you choose to believe? The Bible warns us about changing the Word of God (Deuteronomy 4:2, 12:32; Proverbs 60:6; Revelation 22:18–19). We cannot change the Word of

God to make it what we believe; we must passionately believe what the Word of God says is true.

As Clinton and Jeff Arnold shared,

> The Bible is an amazing and remarkable book. There has never been a book like it. What sets it apart from any other book is that it is God's word for us. We can trust it completely because it is from God and, therefore, without error.[89]

The Bible is complete and not missing anything; the Word informs us as follows.

> Seek and read from the book of the LORD: Not one of these shall be missing; none shall be without her mate. For the mouth of the LORD has commanded, and his Spirit has gathered them. (Isaiah 34:16 ESV)

Does Sin go Unpunished?

Throughout the Bible, it tells us that sin is punishable because sin leads to death and needs to be atoned. Because sin needs to be atoned, God established sacrifices, as described in the Old Testament. The Book of Leviticus describes the various types of sacrifices and how they were to be performed. The first sacrifice was in the Garden of Eden when God killed an animal (shed blood) and made clothing for Adam and Eve after they sinned (Genesis 3:17–21). The sacrifices were to include

---

[89] Arnold, *Short Answers to BIG Questions*, 32.

blood—the blood was used as an atonement to cover our sins. In the New Testament, Jesus is the final blood sacrifice. Sacrifices were established by God, as He is a "just" and "righteous" God. The Bible portrays God's immense love for us, tells us that we are sinners, that sin must be punished, and that we need redemption. Because of the gravity of sin and the result of eternal punishment that God wanted to save us from, was the sole reason that Jesus came to earth to die—to be an atonement for our sins (Ephesian 1:7).

In Chapter 1, I mentioned two questions that Moritz stated in his article. I will answer them at this time.

Are we going to be Thinking of our Loved Ones Suffering in Hell?

The following question is a difficult and sensitive one to answer. Do you feel that you will think of your loved ones and others in the lake of fire while you are in heaven, and thus your life in heaven will be tormented? There are many schools of thought on this; however, I will concentrate on three. Let's study this.

First, there is a consensus that God would not have an eternal hell for unbelievers because believers would be thinking of them while in heaven; subsequently, our eternity in heaven would be miserable—God just would not do that.

Secondly, some believe we will not be thinking of those in the lake of fire because God loves His children dearly (John 16:27 NLT); further, He will be wiping away every tear (Revelation

21:4 NASB). Third, a scripturally sound interpretation is we will know of the unbelievers' torment because of the glory revealed to us (Romans 8:18 ESV). Now, we will examine God's Word to show us the answer.

> Yet what we suffer now is nothing compared to the glory he will reveal to us later. (Romans 8:18 NLT)

> For I consider that the sufferings of this present time are not worth comparing with the glory that is to be revealed to us. (Romans 8:18 ESV)

> When Christ, who is our life, is revealed, then you also will be revealed with Him in glory. (Colossians 3:4 NASB)

> For the Father himself loves you dearly because you love me and believe that I came from God. (John 16:27 NLT)

> And He will wipe away every tear from their eyes; and there will no longer be *any* death; there will no longer be *any* mourning, or crying, or pain; the first things have passed away. (Revelation 21:4 NASB)

> ✓ Scripture furthers explains this in Revelation 7:17 and Isaiah 25:8.

I used two different translations for Romans 8:18 to better grasp what this verse is telling us. As I have stated earlier in my book, it is not scripturally justified to take a singular verse to explain a specific theology and perhaps, take it out of context. Instead, I like to compare scripture to make sure we fully understand a particular subject.

The first philosophy I mentioned above is self-explanatory, in that an eternal hell would not exist because God would want our time in heaven to be full of joy.

The second interpretation sounds doctrinally correct, but is it? Revelation 21:4, 7:17, and Isaiah 25:8 tell us God will wipe away every tear, we will have no more pain, and the first things have passed away. And, because God loves us dearly, God would not have us tormented in heaven by thinking of those in hell. We are God's children, and He only wants the best for us. Some believe this translates that we will not be thinking of the unbelievers suffering eternally in the lake of fire. The second and third viewpoint adheres to the doctrine of eternal punishment in an eternal lake of fire.

The third theology, I believe, stands to the most accurate understanding of God's Word—we will know of the unbelievers' eternal torment. According to scripture in Romans 8:18, our present sufferings are not to be compared to the glory that will be revealed to us. I believe this means how we think about suffering on earth is not to be compared to a revealed knowledge we will receive in heaven. God is pure love and light, full of holiness and righteousness. I have discussed earlier in my book that no sin can come before Him no matter how much He loves us. In keeping with that thought, God is pure good, and He dearly loves His children. When we arrive in heaven, the glory revealed will be a complete understanding of God— His truth and judgment. Colossians 3:4 (NASB) shares that "you also will be revealed with Him [meaning Jesus] in glory." We will know precisely why the unbelievers are in the lake of fire eternally. When in heaven, we will be in a glorified state, not human. Our new understanding will be a Godly one—one of spiritual clarification—not an earthly human perception.

I know from a human perspective the following may seem calloused. But, fundamentally speaking, God's promise of no more tears will be in its most perfect sense in heaven for all believers, for the complete truth and purity of God will be revealed to them. Thus, while in heaven, we will not be eternally mourning the unbelievers' fate in hell, yet we will know of their torment and have a heavenly understanding of God's judgment on them. In Chapter 3, I shared passages from Lamentations and Ezekiel, which showed us that God does not judge willingly, nor does He take pleasure in judging the wicked; He wishes they turn from their evil ways.

Perhaps at first, I believe we will shed tears and mourn for the lost souls, but we must trust God's Word is true—He will wipe away our tears.

POWs Being Tortured Daily

We would never want our loved ones or anyone who has been caught in a war and tortured daily to continue being tortured. We would want to alleviate their pain if we could. But we would probably just want them to die and not suffer any longer. However, soldiers are not in the lake of fire because their names were not in the Book of Life. Sadly, they were captured, and yes, no one wants to have them suffer.

But the lake of fire is not a POW camp. The lake of fire is

torment forever; that is what the Bible says. Therefore, if one's name is not in the Book of Life, God will sentence eternal judgment on that person (Matthew 25:31–46, Revelation 20:15, 21:27) because He is a God of justice and judgment. He is holy and righteous, and unsaved sinners cannot come before Him. According to the Bible, people are wicked and immoral, and because of our humanness, we seem to have a difficult time comprehending that concept. This feeling may indeed be quite daunting, and thus we want to ignore it or disregard it; however, we need to trust what the Bible teaches us—The only way to come before God is redemption through Jesus Christ (John 3:16 and John 14:6)

God gave us His Son to save us from eternal judgment. It is our free-will choice to accept or reject the salvation offered to us. We cannot use our emotions to change the Word of God or try to prove that the lake of fire is complete annihilation or a purification process. Our emotional humanness should not interpret the Bible to fit what we choose to believe; instead, we need to believe what the Bible says. If the Bible states "eternal," then that is what the Bible says.

You Cannot Have It Both Ways

You cannot have one without the other. There cannot be eternal life for those whose names are in the Book of Life without eternal punishment for those whose names are not. Those who believe in the gospel of our Lord will enter the kingdom of God, and those who do not believe will enter the eternal lake of fire.

Unfortunately, unbelievers (and may include our loved ones)

chose to reject the gospel of Jesus Christ. If you are a believer, you accepted the gospel and will enter the kingdom of God. However, your loved ones who choose not to believe and other unbelievers will not enter the kingdom of God; the Word of God is clear on that (Daniel 12:2, Matthew 25:31–46, John 5:29, John 14:6, and Revelation 20:15, 21:27).

We must earnestly pray that our unsaved loved ones will come to know the Lord before they die. Prayer is powerful, and God listens to our prayers. However, everyone chooses to follow Christ or not.

There is no temporary punishment, which will eventually lead to life in heaven. If there is a temporary punishment, there would also have to be temporary rewards in heaven. The scriptures do not teach either situation. Therefore, both heaven and the lake of fire are real with an eternal destination of one's soul.

Let us now look at what Jesus said.

> Strive to enter through the narrow door; for many, I tell you, will seek to enter and will not be able. Once the head of the house gets up and shuts the door, and you begin standing outside and knocking on the door, saying, 'Lord, open up to us!' and He *then* will answer and say to you, 'I do not know where you are from.' (Luke 13:24–25 NASB)

Jesus also spoke of unforgiveness.

> Therefore I tell you, every sin and blasphemy will be forgiven people, but the blasphemy against the

Spirit will not be forgiven. And whoever speaks a word against the Son of Man will be forgiven, but whoever speaks against the Holy Spirit will not be forgiven, either in this age or in the age to come. (Matthew 12:31–32 ESV)

People Choose Their Soul's Eternal Destination

Most people do not sit at a table and ponder their souls' destination. I think most people do not believe in souls, much less an eternal destination after their physical life has ended. I feel that people believe in random birth, life, and death. They plan their lives, education, careers, and even perhaps their funerals. But do they think about their life after death?

Living a life randomly, with no purpose, or should I say with no spiritual meaning, would be living a life of total hopelessness. God's love offers hope to the world through the Holy Spirit.

and hope does not disappoint, because the love of God has been poured out within our hearts through the Holy Spirit who was given to us. (Romans 5:5 NASB)

I do not believe that people accept that they are condemned since Adam and Eve fell into sin in the Garden of Eden (Genesis 3:17–19). Since that moment, humanity has been lost in a state of hopelessness. I feel people do not believe they are sinners per se or in need of redemption. People think they are "good" because they go to work, pay their bills, file their taxes, obey traffic laws, and so on. What do you mean they are going to the lake of fire for eternal punishment? Unfortunately, being a good person will not get you into heaven. Fortunately, however, through our decision to follow Jesus Christ, we will get into heaven.

We can have a hard time grappling with the concepts of sin and hell. We just do not want to believe we are evil, and we do not want to think that a loving God would sentence people to such a horrible place for eternity.

> He repays everyone for what they have done,
> he brings on them what their conduct deserves.
> (Job 34:11 NIV)

> And with you, Lord, is unfailing love; and, You reward everyone according to what they have done. (Psalms 62:12 NIV)

DeStefano describes for us the following.

> God desires no one to go to hell. There is absolutely no sin in the world that can't be forgiven, except final impenitence, that is, the sin of not wanting to be forgiven. That is the unpardonable sin against the Holy Spirit that Christ spoke about in the Gospels.[90]

The following are scriptural examples:

---

[90] DeStefano, *hell (a guide),*183.

> Therefore I tell you, every sin and blasphemy will be forgiven people, but the blasphemy against the Spirit will not be forgiven. (Matthew 12:31 ESV)

> Who wants all people to be saved and to come to a knowledge of the truth. (1 Timothy 2:4 NIV)

> The Lord is not slow in keeping his promise, as some understand slowness. Instead he is patient with you, not wanting anyone to perish, but everyone to come to repentance. (2 Peter 3:9 NIV)

✓ Additional scripture: Mark 3:29; Luke 12:10

If you do not believe, you cannot be saved. Throughout time, humanity has rejected God. God sent several prophets telling people to stop their evil, detestable ways, or XYZ will happen. Did they listen? No, they kept up their wickedness, and sure enough, XYZ happened. Then they shouted, "Why, Lord?" The people of Judah learned a great lesson. They did not stop their evil ways, including worshiping idols. The prophet Jeremiah warned them to turn from their wicked ways (Jeremiah 4:1–8; 20:4–6), but they did not listen. As a result, many were slaughtered, the temple was destroyed, and others were captured and taken off to Babylon for seventy years.

Scripture warns us,

> But because of your stubbornness and unrepentant heart you are storing up wrath for

yourself on the day of wrath and revelation of the
righteous judgment of God. (Romans 2:5 NASB)

Even in current and future times, people reject God. For example, revelation 9 describes war, death, disease, famine, and plagues. Yet, people continued to reject God instead of saying, "Help us, Lord!"

God's divine wrath is the judgment of eternal punishment in the eternal fire for unbelievers—of their own free will. If you are not for God, you are for Satan. There are no gray areas and no picket fences to balance yourself. You can choose to live eternally with God in heaven by redemption through God's Son, Jesus Christ, or you can choose to suffer forever with Satan in the eternal fire—eternally separated from God. I became a believer in Jesus when I was nine years old because of a sermon I heard by Billy Graham. He told us that Jesus loves us, even me. I chose to go to heaven because Jesus loves me, not because there was an eternal hell.

I learned about hell when I was young. My parents taught us the severity of the lake of fire in age-appropriate stages and used examples to help us understand. One such example was: We would never be able to complete an extremely frustrating task while burning in an unquenchable fire. For example, my mom shared that hell for her would be the following: Trying to sew a zipper and it never is correctly done, and having to do it over and over again while her whole body was burning. Granted, not a peaceful thought for a young person, yet very convincing. Recently, my mother shared that she has a greater concept of hell after many years of studying the bible than she did when I was a child. Therefore, reinforcing the more knowledge we acquire from God's Word regarding the lake of fire, we learn that it will be far worse than we can imagine.

There are probably many of you who would think that what my parents did was awful, yet it is the responsibility of Christian parents to instruct their children in the ways of the Lord. The salvation of the parents does not cover others, including children. Every person needs to have a relationship with Jesus. People also need to understand that there are consequences for unforgiven sins. The reality of an eternal lake of fire exists whether you choose to believe it or not.

Oh, by the way, just a note of interest. All five of us children made it through to adulthood well-adjusted (i.e., not traumatized) by knowledge of the lake of fire as children. Our parents told us of the love of God and redemption through Jesus Christ. Everything they told us was from the truth of scripture—it was balanced. Additionally, we all still believe, even in our sixties!

Most importantly, before you speak to your children about heaven and hell, pray first. Then, ask the Lord to lead your conversation for their level of understanding, and always talk about the truth of God's word.

The future also holds the upcoming Tribulation and the destiny for those who reject Jesus Christ. Author, Heitzig explains:

> The destiny for people who reject Jesus Christ during the Tribulation will be exactly the same as for those who reject Jesus Christ at any other time in history: hell.[91]

---

[91] Taken from page 154, *You Can Understand the Book of Revelation*, Copyright © 2011/2020 by Skip Heitzig. Published by Harvest House Publishers, Eugene, Oregon 97408. www.harvesthousepublishers.com.

If you are an unbeliever, I ask you this: Won't you seriously consider your soul's eternal destination? Jesus loves you too!

Heaven or Hell? Your Choice!

Your soul's ultimate destination is in your hands. Only through Jesus Christ can you gain salvation and enter heaven, but there is a time limit for choosing salvation. People sing songs and watch movies that portray there is always a tomorrow, but there is not always a tomorrow—for some, today will be their last day. You can decide to accept Christ while you are alive but only while you are alive. So do not be late with your choice. Jesus is waiting for your response.

> Behold, I stand at the door and knock; if anyone
> hears My voice and opens the door, I will come
> in to him and will dine with him, and he with Me.
> (Revelation 3:20 NASB)

Salvation is a gift from God through belief in Jesus Christ, and our reward is eternal life in heaven with Him. We cannot earn it, work for it, or go through a purification process to receive it. God is not a cruel God; He is a loving God, and He gave us His Son to redeem us, but only if we accept Him as our Lord and Savior. Scripture tells us,

> "… and are justified by his grace as a gift, through
> the redemption that is in Christ Jesus." (Romans
> 3:24 ESV)

In Him, we have redemption through his blood, the forgiveness of our trespasses, according to the riches of his grace. (Ephesians 1:7 ESV)

✓ Additional verses: Colossians 1:14; Hebrews 9:15; 1 Corinthians 1:30

God is a balanced God, as I described in Chapter 2. His nature and character are balanced, and His attributes cannot contradict each other. Yet, to maintain His holiness and righteousness, He is also a God of justice and judgment. Think about what Jesus gave up. Jesus was part of the Triune God and had an exalted status—Jesus became sin to save the world—because He loves us.

In my introduction section, I shared a statement that Moritz had said, "that you have to look at the entire Bible and what it says, and you need to consider the nature and character of God."[92] Moritz is correct, and I agree with him. I have shown you throughout this book how important that statement is in proving that God loves us, Jesus died for us, and our eternal soul's destination—heaven or hell—depends on having a relationship with Jesus Christ or not before we take our last breath. Through scripture, I have also proven that heaven and the lake of fire are eternal; neither one is symbolic (metaphorical). Together, along with the above, we learned that the lake of fire is not complete annihilation, nor is it a purification process.

An uplifting thought: We can determine through scripture what heaven is all about, yet we may not fully understand our rewards and the concept of eternity. The truth is we know

---

[92] Moritz, *Hell.*

where we are going, and because of our redemption through Jesus Christ, we will confidently know Who we are going with.

The scriptural documentation I have presented lets us know precisely why—my fellow journey takers—we absolutely need Jesus Christ as our Lord and Savior.

I sincerely pray that you have discovered through your journey with me that "God so loved the world that he gave his only begotten Son, that whosoever believeth in Him should not perish but have everlasting life" (John 3:16 KJV).

EPILOGUE—TO WRAP THINGS UP

God did give us an out from His justice of the lake of fire through His mercy through His Son, Jesus Christ.

God's message of love and redemption is vital to all persons. His message is in His Word, which explains the importance of the death and resurrection of His only begotten Son, Jesus Christ.

Jesus made an immense sacrifice on your behalf—this act set us free from our sins—if we only believe.

If you have not done so already, take the precious time you have right now and ask Jesus to be the Lord of your life.

I encourage you to continue your journey. Keep reading your Bible, keep praying, and stay in touch with your Lord.

Always remember, "The grass withers, the flower fades, But the word of our God stands forever." (Isaiah 40:8 NASB).

Spiritual Awareness Questions

I asked the following questions earlier.

> Jesus asked His disciples, "'But who do you say that I am?' Peter answered and said to Him, 'You are the Christ'" (Mark 8:29 NASB)

✓ See also Matthew 16:15, Luke 9:20.

If Jesus Christ asked you that same question, what would your response be?

Is your name in the Book of Life? What does your eternity look like?

The following passage is speaking of who will enter the Kingdom of God.

Nothing evil will be allowed to enter, nor anyone who practices shameful idolatry and dishonesty—but only those whose names are written in the Lamb's Book of Life. (Revelation 21:27 NLT)

Was your response the same as earlier, or did you have a change of heart?

And this I pray, that your love may overflow still more and more in real knowledge and all discernment, so that you may discover the things that are excellent, that you may be sincere and blameless for the day of Christ; having been filled with the fruit of righteousness which *comes* through Jesus Christ, for the glory and praise of God. (Philippians 1:9–11 NASB)

Finally, brothers *and sisters*, pray for us that the word of the Lord will spread rapidly and be glorified, just as *it was* also with you. (2 Thessalonians 3:1 NASB)

One final question:

Can you raise your hands to God and say,
"I Worship You!"?

Thank you for taking this journey with me, and I sincerely hope your road of discovery led you to truthful answers to your questions.

PART FOUR

A Biblical Overview for Continued Growth

A SPECIAL MESSAGE FROM ELISABETH

Dear Reader,

I sensitively and lovingly share this special message. I invite you from the depths of my heart and soul to consider salvation through Jesus Christ.

- God loves everyone and allows everyone to receive redemption through His Son, Jesus Christ (John 3:16).
- What everyone needs to understand is that we are all sinners (Romans 3:23), and the "wages of sin is death" (Romans 6:23 ESV); thus, we all need redemption (1 John 1:9, John 3:16 and John 14:6).
- As sinners, we cannot come before God and be received into heaven no matter how much God loves us unless we have been redeemed by Jesus Christ of our own free will.
- When we accept redemption, we become saved sinners and can come before God. Our names are added to the Book of Life when we receive Jesus Christ as our Savior; therefore, we will not be thrown into the lake of fire (Revelation 20:15). Praise the Lord!
- Jesus' death on the cross paid the price (a ransom/ rescued us, Matthew 20:28; Galatians 1:4; 1 Timothy

2:6; 1 Peter 1:18–21), the penalty for our sins, which showed us His sacrificial love for us.

- However, there is a time limit to accepting the offer of salvation. We need to make our decision before our death (Hebrews 9:27). There are no postmortem opportunities for redemption, for we will be held accountable/without an excuse (Romans 1:20).

I tenderly ask you to accept the gift of salvation if you have not already done so. You do not need to do any deeds—only ask the Lord Jesus to forgive you of your sins and come into your heart today. Jesus is waiting for your response.

If you made your decision to follow Christ, you are now a child of God. He is the father to the fatherless and protects widows (Psalms 68:5 NIV). He is "the helper of the fatherless." (Psalms 10:14 NIV) Praise the Lord!

"Therefore, everyone who confesses Me before people, I will also confess him before My Father who is in heaven." (Matthew 10:32 NASB)

"…I tell you, there is joy in the presence of the angels of God over one sinner who repents." (Luke 15:10 NASB)

But as many as received Him, to them He gave the right to become children of God, to those who believe in His name. (John 1:12 NASB)

However, you are not in the flesh but in the Spirit, if indeed the Spirit of God dwells in you. But if anyone does not have the Spirit of Christ, he does not belong to Him. (Romans 8:9 NASB)

If Christ is in you, though the body is dead because of sin, yet the spirit is alive because of righteousness. (Romans 8:10 NASB)

Additionally, when you become a child of God, an extraordinary event happens—the Holy Spirit moves into your life. You now have a teacher and a helper. Also, you have a spiritual daddy, the Abba Father. As I have grown spiritually, I have learned how vital the Holy Spirit is. I feel that I perhaps learned too late, for there have been times I should have relied on my Abba Father more often. We cannot make up time with God for our past; we must move forward with a new commitment. God sees our hearts, and I am thankful. Praise the Lord!

- ✓ Scripture on Abba Father: Mark 14:36, Romans 8:15, Galatians 4:5–7

That is the main reason I wrote this book: To share the Gospel message of God's love and truth so that all may share in the wonderful event with the Abba Father. There are no human words to describe it, as it is truly spiritual.

The Arnolds shared an important message of encouragement that the Bible offers to all persons.

We discover him by pouring over the pages of scripture. It is there that he meets us and reveals himself to us. And we can trust the Bible. It is accurate and reliable. It is also incredibly powerful to change our lives because God's Spirit works through it.[93]

Additionally, when we become children of God, we are now responsible for sharing the message with others; therefore, becoming a light unto a dark world. Matthew 5:14 tells us, "You are the light of the world—like a city on a hilltop that cannot be hidden" (NLT).

Perhaps we will meet someday and know we are brothers and sisters in Christ, and if we do not get to meet in this life, I will see you in heaven. Oh, what a glorious day it will be when we meet our Lord, amen!

Remember, God loves you too! Yes, even you!
With God, "All life matters!"

This is not the end nor a final goodbye; it is a farewell for now. I hope to see you on my next journey. I have two planned adventures through scripture coming up, or perhaps more—God willing! In the meantime, I will send you off with this inspiration.

And now, just as you accepted Christ Jesus as your Lord, you must continue to follow him. Let your roots grow down into him, and let your lives

---

[93] Arnold, *Short Answers to BIG Questions*, 355.

be built on him. Then your faith will grow strong in the truth you were taught, and you will overflow with thankfulness. (Colossians 2:6–7 NLT)

In His Service,
Elisabeth C. Nelson

BENEDICTIONS—BLESSINGS BE UPON YOU

Selected Benedictions from the Bible

Fear thou not, for I am with thee: be not dismayed; for I am thy God: I will strengthen thee; yea, I will help thee; yea, I will uphold thee with the right hand of my righteousness. (Isaiah 41:10 KJV)

Now may the God of peace Himself sanctify you entirely; and may your spirit and soul and body be kept complete, without blame at the coming of our Lord Jesus Christ. (1 Thessalonians 5:23 NASB)

But we are bound to give thanks alway to God for you, brethren beloved of the Lord, because God hath from the beginning chosen you to salvation through sanctification of the Spirit and belief of the truth: Whereunto he called you by our gospel, to the obtaining of the glory of our Lord Jesus Christ. Therefore, brethren, stand fast, and hold the traditions which ye have been taught, whether by word, or our epistle. Now our Lord Jesus Christ himself, and God, even our

Father, which hath loved us, and hath given us everlasting consolation and good hope through grace, Comfort your hearts, and stablish you in every good word and work. (2 Thessalonians 2:13–17 KJV)

At my first defense no one supported me, but all deserted me; may it not be counted against them. But the Lord stood with me and strengthened me, so that through me the proclamation might be fully accomplished, and that all the Gentiles might hear; and I was rescued out of the lion's mouth. The Lord will rescue me from every evil deed, and will bring me safely to His heavenly kingdom; to Him *be* the glory forever and ever. Amen. (2 Timothy 4:16–18 NASB)

Now the God of peace, that brought again from the dead our Lord Jesus, that great shepherd of the sheep, through the blood of the everlasting covenant, Make you perfect in every good work to do his will, working in you that which is wellpleasing in his sight, through Jesus Christ; to whom be glory for ever and ever. Amen. (Hebrews 13:20–21 KJV)

… so that the tested genuineness of your faith—more precious than gold that perishes though it is tested by fire—may be found to result in praise and glory and honor at the revelation of Jesus Christ. (1 Peter 1:7 ESV)

… but grow in the grace and knowledge of our Lord and Savior Jesus Christ. To Him *be* the glory, both now and to the day of eternity. Amen. (2 Peter 3:18 NASB)

To him who is able to keep you from stumbling and to present you before his glorious presence without fault and with great joy—to the only God our Savior be glory, majesty, power and authority, through Jesus Christ our Lord, before all ages, now and forevermore! Amen. (Jude 24–25 NIV)

He who testifies to these things says, "Yes, I am coming quickly." Amen. Come, Lord Jesus. The grace of the Lord Jesus be with all. Amen. (Revelation 22:20–21 NASB)

Jesus gave us the Lord's Prayer as an outline and guide of what our prayers should include. It is not meant to be viewed or used as a mantra, yet it is an important passage. Jesus wants our prayers to be from our heart to His heart.

The Lord's Prayer

After this manner therefore pray ye:
Our Father which art in heaven,
Hallowed be thy name.
Thy kingdom come, Thy will be done
in earth, as it is in heaven.
Give us this day our daily bread.
And forgive us our debts,
as we forgive our debtors.
And lead us not into temptation,
but deliver us from evil:
For thine is the kingdom, and the power,
and the glory, for ever. Amen.
(Matthew 6:9–13 KJV)

FOR FURTHER READING—
TO ASSIST YOU ON YOUR JOURNEY

The following booklist includes all books used for reference material and additional books that I felt might interest you.

30 Life Principles: A Study for Growing in Knowledge and Understanding of God
Charles F. Stanley
(Nashville: Thomas Nelson, 2008).

40 Questions about Heaven and Hell
Alan W. Gomes
(Grand Rapids: Kregel Academics, 2018).

Angels, Revised
Billy Graham
(Nashville: Thomas Nelson, 1996).

Angels: Who They Are and How They Help…What the Bible Reveals
David Jeremiah
(New York City: Random House, 2009).

Bible Revival: Recommitting Ourselves to One Book
Kenneth Berding
(Wooster: Weaver Book Company, 2013).
[Lexham Publishing purchased Weaver Books]

Four Views On Hell
Preston Sprinkle, Denny Burk, John Stackhouse Jr., Robin Parry, and Jerry Walls.
(Grand Rapids: Zondervan, 2016).

Heaven
Randy Alcorn
(Carol Stream: Tyndale House, 2004).

hell (a guide)
Anthony DeStefano
(Nashville: Nelson Books, 2020).

How to Live an "In Christ" Life: 100 Devotional Readings on Union with Christ
Kenneth Berding
(Geanies House, Fearn, Scotland: Christian Focus Publications, 2020).

Knowing Grace: Cultivating a Lifestyle of Godliness
Joanne J. Jung
(Downers Grove: InterVarsity Press, 2011).

Short Answers to BIG Questions about God, the Bible & Christianity
Clinton E. Arnold and Jeff Arnold
(Grand Rapids: Baker Books, 2015).

The Case for Christ
Lee Strobel
(Grand Rapids: Zondervan, 1998, 2016).

The Cross, 13 Studies for Individuals or Groups
John Stott
(Downers Grove: InterVarsity Press, 2009).

The Forgotten Trinity
James R. White
(Bloomington: Bethany House, 1998).

The Hole in our Gospel
Richard Stearns
(Nashville: W. Publishing Group, an imprint of Thomas Nelson, 2009, 2010, 2014, 2019).

Trinity and Humanity: An introduction to the Theology of Colin Gunton
Uche Anizor
(Milton Keynes, UK: Paternoster, 2016).

Two Views of Hell
Edward William Fudge and Robert A. Peterson
(Downers Grove: InterVarsity Press, 2000).

When We Say Father
Stephen M. Rodgers and Adrian Rogers
(Nashville: B&H Publishing, 2018).

Who Is Jesus? 66 Great Names and Titles Explained and Applied
Paul Kent
(Uhrichsville: Barbour Books, 2020).

You Can Understand the Book of Revelation: Exploring Its Mystery and Message
Skip Heitzig
(Eugene: Harvest House, 2011, 2020).

… and don't forget the Holy Bible.

PRO-LIFE RESOURCES AND ADVOCATES

Below is a brief list of resources to help those who may have questions regarding pregnancy choices or increase their knowledge about pro-life advocacy.

Dr. James Dobson Family Institute
Home of Family Talk
Pro-Life Advocates
www.drjamesdobson.org

Obria Medical Clinics
Pro-Life Pregnancy Care Clinics
Pregnancy and STD Testing
Ultrasounds and Post-Abortion Counseling
www.obria.org

Pacific Justice Institute
Christian Attorneys
Advancing Religious Freedom
Pro-Life Advocates
www.pji.org

Pre-Born!

"Save babies and souls."
Pro-Life Advocates and Post-Abortion Resources
https.//preborn.org

Susan B. Anthony List

Pro-Life Advocates with a Mission
to end Abortion
www.sbalist.org

Women Speak Out PAC

A partner of Susan B. Anthony List
"Amplifying the voices of women opposed to abortion extremists
in Congress."
www.sba-list.org/women-speak-out-pac

For a continuous [per second] count on how many abortions were performed, whether in the United States or worldwide, visit: www.numberofabortions.com

The statistics are generated voluntarily from agencies and consist of recorded abortions only. Therefore, abortions performed before the dates given, unreported abortions, or abortions illegally performed are not included in the totals.

Adapted from an Upcoming Article by Elisabeth C. Nelson

Afraid for America!

An Overview

I have heard many times throughout my life that "if you are not part of the solution, you are part of the problem." The following message is my part of offering a solution to our country's dilemma. Our country is heading for disaster.

It appears that Americans will soon lose something they all cherish—"liberty for all."

Additionally, America has lost something precious—Honoring God. America has taken God out of its schools, has taken Him out of the courtrooms by removing the Ten Commandments, and removing "Under God" from the pledge of allegiance. I hear that we may be removing "In God We Trust" from our currency.

I am afraid for our world because many nations have already suffered from the following plights. Our country has a triple whammy on its head. Every country that has taken God out of its infrastructure—the family—eventually has fallen from its greatness. The government is not necessarily weak *per se*, for tyranny is a negative strength, and hence, freedom no longer exists. Its power does not always determine a country's greatness. Greatness is related to how a country functions—Honoring God or not throughout and within the family and the government. When the family's morals deteriorate, this translates into our judicial system members' decisions. I thank the Lord God above for judges and lawmakers who base their conclusions on a conservative and faith-based view. We need judges and lawmakers that put honoring God first in their decisions instead of pleasing people. The end times are on the horizon, which evil governments will become great, yet they will ultimately fail.

3 Potential Curses on America's Head

The curses are already underway in our country because our morals and our original high standards of how America functioned have diminished. Curses come in many shapes and forms, and the timing is not always immediate. Results of not honoring God could be in the form of war, disease, famine, earthquakes, floods, or plagues, or even overthrown governments. Many countries worldwide are currently experiencing them. Additionally, there is an imminent worldwide curse headed our way: Shedding of Innocent Blood. This worldwide curse is discussed in Chapter 4 and is another upcoming article.

Curse 1: Not Supporting Israel.

Genesis 12:1–3 explains that if anyone blesses Abraham (Israel) will be blessed, and those who curse him will be cursed. Abraham is the father of Israel (Genesis 12:7, Acts 7:2–8). If our administration sides with Iran and other Israel's enemies, our nation will be cursed.

Solution: America needs to stand behind and assist Israel.

I encourage other countries in our world to do the same. Honoring God needs to come first. Just remember, the Jewish people are the "apple of God's eyes" (Zechariah 2:8 NASB). Yet, additionally, since Jesus died for our sins, all believers are God's children. Some may feel that since the Jewish religion and nation has rejected Jesus as the Messiah, they should be on their own. I'm afraid I have to disagree with that philosophy. I prefer to be part of a country that honors God and not negate the responsibility to protect and support Israel.

Curse 2: Socialism

All Americans need to fight to keep the entrepreneurship spirit alive! I have read success stories in various business magazines that tell how several individuals started their companies in their garages in the past years. Or portrayed entrepreneurs who perhaps slept on a friend's sofa while they poured all their monies into their business. Their sacrifices finally paid off, and some now have companies that employ tens of thousands of people. With Socialism, those companies will be owned and operated by the government. Some socialistic countries allow small "Mom and Pop" businesses to function independently, yet larger corporations will be under the state and local governments. To those who fought long and hard for your business to become successful, "are you going to allow the government to take that away from you?"

For the benefit of many, I will explain Socialism and what will most likely happen to our country in simple basic terms. But, unfortunately, many fellow Americans want to steer the American people toward Socialism, and many of them are our lawmakers.

Socialism is on the brink of our shores and maybe heading our way sooner than some have speculated. Every country that has turned to Socialism has fallen from its prominence. There are mainly two class distinctions: the very wealthy and the poverty-stricken. Unfortunately, the poverty level works only for the benefit of the country under government control. Socialistic leaders do not care about the individual's dreams or aspirations. Entrepreneurship/private industry is no longer encouraged or allowed; hence, Capitalism will no longer exist.

Those in charge do not care if you get a better house, a better car, etc. If an enhanced education benefits the country, that will be encouraged, but your individual goals are of no concern. It will not happen overnight, as it is a gradual process. To my best understanding, Venezuela is a more recent country that has turned to Socialism and has deteriorated from its once greatness.

A crucial factor, Socialism is evil and is spawned by Satan, which sponsors another tragedy. Under Socialism will be the abolishment of Christian churches and Christian schools. Socialism does not encourage the worshiping of God and is punishable by imprisonment or death. So much for freedom of religion, which was one of the main reasons our country was established (colonized). Our forefathers came to a new land to *escape* tyranny, *create* freedom for all, and *embrace* religious freedom—this includes worshiping God.

Further, many people in our country scream and yell "tolerance." Really? Then why is the country as a whole not tolerant of Christians? The world, in general, is not susceptible to Christians because the world hates Christians. Why does the world hate Christians? It is because the Christian faith is mutually exclusive. God, the Bible, and the Christian faith are offensive to the world. Therefore, the world considers the Christian faith a "hate group." I think the reverse is more accurate—the world is a hate group that hates Christians. In short, mutually exclusive means there is only one way out—that is, through Jesus! The world hates and rejects this concept, and therefore the world hates those who believe in it. Yes, the Gospel of Jesus Christ is exclusive yet inclusive for all who believe it! There is no greater love because God is for you!

Initially, our country's constitution did not suggest or advocate the separation of church and state—we used to be One Nation Under God. Unfortunately, the liberal judges of our judicial system have hacked our constitution to change its original meaning. Further, Socialism is "anti-faith, anti-family, and anti-freedom."[94] Dobson also stated, "The Judeo-Christian system of values that have upheld our great nation for nearly 250 years is in danger of disintegrating."[95] Scripture defines freedom as an opportunity to "serve one another through love" (Galatians 5:13 NASB). Our lawmakers need to go back to "We the people" and serve those people with God's love in all their governing decisions. Now, that is an America I would be proud to be a citizen! Hear! Hear!

In the beginning, a majority of the population will *run* to and *embrace* Socialism. The leaders who introduce a "new government order" to change America fundamentally will give charismatic speeches. The leaders will be informing people that there is no discrimination by promoting that everyone will be considered and treated equally. Speeches will portray and assure the population that the government will take care of them. In essence, people get in the habit of standing in line for "free goodies" and, unknowingly, are willing to give up their freedom for it.

Let's examine things for a moment. It starts with a short line for free food. Then, the line stretches with free phones. The line grows further with waiving evictions, for there is much fraud within this program. I understand that the pandemic has caused

---

[94] Dr. James Dobson Family Institute, email article, *Georgia Runoff Race Becomes Ground Zero* (December 7, 2020).

[95] Ibid.

a financial crisis in many families. However, some abuse the program to get out of paying their rent without an eviction. But with the tighter criteria, it makes it tougher to avoid paying your rent and not be qualified to do so. My favorite point to make is the enormously lengthy line for those who receive the $600 per week extra on unemployment. To my best understanding, it is speculated that those receiving the extra $600 a week are making more than when they were working. No wonder that millions upon millions of people are on unemployment.

Where is the incentive to work? I know the job market in some careers are shut down or limited; however, there are comparable jobs open; why don't they change or shift careers? I also understand that there is a tremendous amount of fraud, and the EDD employees are cyphering through that mess. Further, the IRS taxes unemployment income, and some states, making it costly at tax time. Innovative individuals will live within their means and save what they can of the extra money. I understand there was a change from $600 to $300. As of this writing (February 2021), the new stimulus package advocates $400 per week but has not yet been approved. No matter the weekly rate, there is still a tax burden.

I am not insensitive to the current plight of unemployment, as I have been in that state a few times throughout my life. However, there were times I chose to work for a temporary employment agency instead of signing up for unemployment; at least the taxes were taken out of my paycheck. Additionally, a person usually makes more money working as a temp than on unemployment. Like me, I know others who are bottom-line thinkers as we analyze the best option for the long run, not the short run. Moreover, I have had to change careers or industries several times to keep working. Sometimes you have to bite the financial bullet or grin and bear it to benefit a long-term positive outcome.

The habit of receiving handouts promotes and leads to a dependence on the government instead of developing independence. Additionally, over some time, people start adopting an attitude of entitlement. One of the essential points I am making is this: if the government stops the "free stuff," what will you do? Do you have a backup plan to support yourself? In all actuality, the government is building its future workforce for the "new government order." Have you ever been fishing? You put either artificial bait or a worm on the hook's end to attract a fish and lower the line into the water. Walla! The fish gets nabbed. In other words, people are being reeled in with free stuff; unknowingly, they are being recruited as a workforce—virtually selling their souls to the government.

The leaders will also give captivating news about improving our country as the Utopia we only dream about to sell Socialism. Most likely, they may not use the word "Socialism;" they will camouflage it. Some examples are *let's unite together as patriots*, or *it's your patriotic duty.* Those statements in themselves are not wrong, but when you perhaps have a mindset of uniting together as one, forgetting about the differences between the political parties of red and blue, that paints a different picture—The picture being one of Socialism, not democracy! Further, the unity I am hearing is that we need to side with one particular viewpoint and not oppose it. That standpoint does not appear to be one of democracy or freedom. Additionally, "a new government order" sounds very familiar to "a new world order" by Hitler! Do we ever learn our lessons from history?

With Socialism, there is also abolishing freedom of speech, which is currently happening in our country. Between December 2020 and early 2021, various social media companies are censoring and suspending/closing accounts expressing opinions about election fraud, pro-Trump remarks, or speaking against the new administration. For example, an Internet article posted on January 17, 2021: Twitter Suspends US Congresswoman Over Election Fraud Claims.[96] As a result, some Republican lawmakers who defended Trump are politically attacked and threatened with their university degrees revoked. Why? This kind of censorship leads to Socialism/Communism.

Further, censorship has already happened on the various social media accounts regarding moral issues on posted comments or articles against homosexuality and abortion, or even pro-Trump comments. Why? Are the news media and lawmakers afraid of people learning the truth? It comes down to this—if everyone knows the "real" truth about the changes in our governmental structure, they will see when the lawmakers are developing wrong decisions for our country; thus, we will fight back. Additionally, is portraying independent thought now illegal? Homosexuality and abortion are not Biblically sanctioned. To take it one step further, if all women decided to keep their babies, what would happen to the abortion industry? I believe I made one of my points.

On a more progressive note, I would like to submit a resolution to the abortion industry. Just think about the positive and substantial impact you would make on our country and further set a precedent to the world if you would channel your funds and focus on saving lives instead of murdering babies.

____

[96] Article from Associated Press, by Sophia Tulp, retrieved on January 17, 2021.

Just because abortion is legal does not make it Biblically legal. If laws are contrary to scripture, then those laws are wrong. Your clinics and funds could advance research to save lives, offer social services, parenting and sexual abstinence training classes, or assist with adoption services. Another possibility is cancer research for children. Wow! What an impact and legacy! Abortionists, are you up for the challenge?

Some believe there will be equal pay. Well, here is some food for thought: A Ph.D. receives the same wages as a food worker. Is that what everyone wants? The truth is this; the government pays a wage they think you are worth, not what you think your value is. Equal pay only produces a diminished incentive to succeed and a weakened sense of competition; thus, why try to achieve? Another way of looking at it, Socialism kills research, and competition dries up. The only equality that exists in Socialism is a majority of people experience being oppressed and impoverished. One day in the future, you will be sitting at your table, if you have one, and think, *what happened to America?* Watch out, America!

One of the primary differences between Capitalism and Socialism is how industry (production and distribution) is managed: With Capitalism, the overall industry is private ownership, whereas industry is owned and operated by the government with Socialism (paraphrased).[97] With Socialism, private healthcare will be replaced with socialized medicine, such as Obamacare or Bidencare. As I stated earlier, there are two main class distinctions; therefore, the middle class no longer exists. Tyranny is part of Socialism, and in time, it will

---

[97] Investopedia, Capitalism vs. Socialism: What's the Difference? Retrieved on 12/20/20.

only increase; the general population will suffer oppression and cruelty.

Even though Socialism vs. Capitalism is more than just about how our economy is managed, it is also about our leadership's political and spiritual viewpoints (i.e., the leadership's moral values). Therefore, in long-term toxic socialistic societies, democracy is abolished and replaced with autocracy, considered a dictatorship—one-party rule. The bottom line—Socialism, Marxism, and Communism are all in one together.

In some socialistic countries, personal property is seized by the state or local governments, including confiscating bank accounts. So, watch out, homeowners; your home may be appropriated altogether or turned into two or three apartments. Or, perhaps, the government will assign people to live with you.

Socialism also promotes a lack of improvement because there is no reward for forward-thinking or achievement. The ongoing diminished incentive eventually causes the population to be emotionally depressed. Depression leads to a lack of growth and overall diminished production; therefore, a once-thriving country stops growing; hence, a country will start experiencing zero-to-negative population growth. This lack of change over time will ultimately turn a prosperous country into a dying nation. Of course, there are different forms and levels of Socialism, so that each socialistic society will experience different outcomes. But, whatever the case, Capitalism is a far better alternative to Socialism.

Along with honoring God, Capitalism has been the driving force that has energized the United States of America's growth and power! Honoring God and working as a Capitalistic society has set America apart and above all other countries. So why do we want to destroy that achievement? If our nation turns to Socialism, we will no longer have our elite status in the world.

Socialism in a nutshell: Every person needs to work for their keep, except perhaps the wealthy. In other words, the poverty-stricken class needs to be productive workers for the government's benefit. If one no longer can earn their keep, they are eliminated, in one-way shape or form. If one is caught worshipping God, they are eliminated as well. The government will dictate which "god" you may worship, usually being the country's leader (as in China) or a government-selected church (as in Russia).

Suppose our country turns into a socialistic society—In that case, our America will no longer be the "land of the free or the land of the opportunity"—the America we have known and loved will no longer exist!

Solution: America needs to fight for continued Private Industry!

A non-violent way to fight is by writing your various senators and representatives to fight for our rights to keep the private industry alive! However, this may not be easy because some of our legislative members are socialists and cannot wait for our society to become a socialistic society. This result happened over numerous years because many Americans voted for them throughout past and current elections. The leaders we voted for will determine and enforce laws regulating which type of governmental structure governs us. Further, our country does not seem to learn from the history of other countries around the world. The movie, *China Cry*,[98] will educate you on how

---

[98] *China Cry,* A TBN Film, Distributed by Vision Video.

bad it can get with a socialistic-communistic society based on a true story.

America works best when all abled-body people work and be part of a productive society; however, families, churches, and governmental programs need to step in and assist with caring for those who no longer cannot work because of mental or physical limitations. Those who are retired should choose to go back to work or not, depending upon their situation.

Our America has functioned and prospered for nearly 250 years as a capitalistic society. America has grown through those years as one of the most significant world powers—unique from all other countries. Therefore, I ask this question: Why do people want to change that? If we convert to Socialism, we will be no better than any other country. Because America has chosen to stop honoring God in its laws and judicial system, and with the addition of Socialism, it will deteriorate—crumble and tumble—as a great nation.

Curse 3: Taking God out of the Equation.

This message is for the world as well, as we are all living in spiritual darkness. When laws are established that are contrary to God's Holy Word, then those laws are wrong. The strength of a country depends upon the strength or weakness of the infrastructure—the family. If the family is weak, then the government will eventually tumble. One of the main reasons the Roman Empire fell was because the family was broken due to the society's decline of Godly morals.

The scriptures remind us:

Therefore, treat the parts of your earthly body as dead *to* sexual immorality, impurity, passion, evil desire, and greed, which amounts to idolatry. (Colossians 3:5 NASB)

We know that our old sinful selves were crucified with Christ so that sin might lose its power in our lives. We are no longer slaves to sin. (Romans 6:6 NLT)

The Romans worshipped their gods instead of God. The family turned to immorality instead of living lives pleasing to God. An excellent book regarding this thesis is *The Decline and Fall of the Roman Empire* by Edward Gibbon. The book was first published in the 18th century. The author's theory of the fall of the Roman Empire was due to "Roman decadence and loss of virtue."[99] The quote was taken from the description of the book on Christianbook.com. Does this seem familiar with what is going on in America? America is heading for destruction because its morals have declined to an all-time low by disregarding Godly values—killing babies and sexual perversion. It appears that America's new morality is—anything goes! Again, I reiterate, we do not seem to learn from the history of other countries, or for that matter, from past world powers that no longer exist or have deteriorated.

The book mentioned above is no longer required reading in our colleges, since the change in our laws and our country's standards and morals have declined. In other words, America is headed for destruction. Matthew 7:13–14 (For complete

---

[99] Edward Gibbon, *The Decline and Fall of the Roman Empire* (New York: Modern Library, 2013), ePub.

scriptural reference, see Chapter 2 under "Do All Roads Lead to the Same Place?"), describes two main paths: "the way is broad that leads to destruction" (v 13 NASB) is one path we need to avoid.

Solution: America and other Countries put God back into the Equation.

We need to put God back into the equation—start honoring God once again—in our homes and throughout the various judicial systems. As I discussed in my Introduction section, God does allow U-Turns!

Start Honoring
God Once Again!

Summation

Moving forward, start honoring God in all your decisions, whether personal, professional, or political. Vote only for the candidates that base their governing decisions that are in line with God's Word.

I heard many impressive speeches on live broadcasts from various lawmakers on the Senate floor on January 6, 2021, expressing that our nation needs to heal and unite as one nation. Well, isn't that original? How about—One Nation under God? That statement explicitly tells us there is no separation of church and state. But I did not hear that from any of our legislators.

Further, many speeches expressed such high regard for democracy, almost in a god-like manner. Indeed, we need to cherish democracy. I love democracy just as much as the next person, but democracy is not a god, nor are we to worship democracy. Additionally, the Senate floor is not a temple or cathedral of democracy—it is a place where legislators conduct the country's business with democracy as a solid base and as One Nation Under God. Yes, indeed, we are to uphold democracy, but we are not to worship it. God is God, and we are to honor Him above all other entities and all things. Scripture informs us, "You shall have no other gods before me" (Exodus 20:3 ESV).

Instead of indoctrinating our young minds from first grade through college on how they should think vs. independent thought, I suggest an alternative. Add patriotic education to our teaching in our schools, such as the Rudiments of our American Government, which is "perceiving the history of Christianity and

America as inseparable and requisite to understanding the relation of individual character to a nation's government."[100] Further, adding to the curriculum the "study of the American Christian constitutional form of government and the idea of liberty with law."[101] And third, a history class covering the "study of Christ: His story, the westward movement of Christianity, Christian liberty, government, and individual character as contrasted with the pagan and socialistic story."[102] Moreover, the schools should teach our students the following principles at every grade level:

- God's Principle of Individuality
- For every ounce of freedom, there is an ounce of responsibility
- One person's rights end when another's begin

Instead, our children are taught that abortion is okay and homosexuality is normal when God's Word teaches the opposite. Moreover, our children need to learn independent thought and make decisions based on sound doctrine and knowledge.

Our legislative system would be 50% to 100% better if our lawmakers applied the following scripture to their political decisions—"Do nothing from selfishness or empty conceit, but with humility consider one another as more important than yourselves; do not *merely* look out for your own personal *interests*, but also for the *interests* of others" (Philippians 2:3–4

---

[100] See my Tribute to American Heritage Christian Schools in my Acknowledgement section.

[101] Ibid.

[102] Ibid.

NASB). This Biblical passage looks remarkably similar to "We the People" in that if there is a problem, those legislators and lawmakers in charge are responsible for making it right for "the People" and not for personal special interests. And, since our forefathers came to America to flee tyranny, why are we heading back to it? Our country's forefathers had the vision and the wisdom to break away from tyranny and create a new way of life, and now we are returning to tyranny after nearly 250 years. Where is the God-given logic?

People are politically attacked, and our freedom of speech in America is no longer a benefit. People talk about unity, yet they want to have us jump aboard their team without opposing them. That mindset sounds like dictatorship, not democracy. Even though I can't entirely agree with all the political views of the various "parties," I love the red and blue political parties, and the other ones too. The various political parties, in part, demonstrate God's principle of individuality, translating those independent thoughts into the freedom of speech. However, I do not believe that God created humankind in His image and likeness, that He had the political parties in mind (Genesis 1:26)—humanity came up with that radical idea. Yet, the different political parties serve the purpose of grouping individual thoughts into factions of similar beliefs. The ultimate unity would be all nations under God working together to please God. Please, someone, tell me why we are censoring freedom of speech and returning to tyranny?

How many of you value freedom? Our military and past veterans fought for our country's independence, and many have died to keep America free. Those who disagree with the Declaration of Independence or the United States of America's

Constitution have the right to move to a different country. The false illusion you have formulated that the government will be taking care of you will surely disappoint you. Since it appears you do not like and appreciate the freedom you have in America, move out! Other countries in our world do not have the independence you have enjoyed in America that you can move to; here are a few suggestions, China, Russia, North Korea, Cuba, and Venezuela. To the leaders in America that promote Socialism, perhaps you can change those other countries, but do not change America; leave her alone!

A spiritual reminder to the Christians worldwide living in tyranny:

> If God is for us, who is against us? (Romans 8:31b NASB)

> For I am persuaded, that neither death, nor life, nor angels, nor principalities, nor powers, nor things present, nor things to come, Nor height, nor depth, nor any other creature, shall be able to separate us from the love of God, which is in Christ Jesus our Lord. (Romans 8:38–39 KJV)

Our country's only channel of healing is through the power of Jesus Christ, for He is the Healer (Exodus 15:26) and our Counselor (Isaiah 9:6). The only true unity is when all American citizens and those enjoying the freedom you have in America join together as One Nation under God. The ultimate unity will be when the world unites as One World under God!

Finishing words that provide our world hope:

The following passage foretold us that our Messiah, Jesus Christ, is coming:

For a Child will be born to us, a Son will be given to us; And the government will rest on His shoulders; And His name will be called Wonderful Counselor, Mighty God, Eternal Father, Prince of Peace. (Isaiah 9:6 NASB)

And, Jesus said,

These things I have spoken unto you, that in me ye might have peace. In the world ye shall have tribulation: but be of good cheer; I have overcome the world. (John 16:33 KJV)

Lightning Source UK Ltd.
Milton Keynes UK
UKHW011923180822
407522UK00008B/229/J